"*The Pastor and the Modern Culture* is a rare gem. Thre writing from his own perspective, offer us instruction and inspiration for fruitful ministry. Here we gain insight into our cultural moment, wisdom for our weekly preaching, and humility from our distant history. I feel privileged to recommend this captivating book."

—RAY ORTLUND, Pastor to Pastors, Immanuel Church, Nashville

"In these lectures, seasoned pastor-theologians equip us to proclaim the epoch-transcending gospel of Christ into a cultural milieu that imagines that it has outgrown such good news. Dr. Edgar insightfully profiles that secular milieu by engaging trends in philosophy, social sciences, and the arts. Dr. Hughes invites us into his pastoral study, showing us how to hear (humbly) and herald (boldly!) God's good message, which stirs affections and transforms hearts. Dr. Poirier challenges us to become men so overwhelmed by our calling to be spiritual physicians that we cast ourselves, in desperation, on the Savior who came to heal sin-sick folk like us. Together, these fathers in the faith—and the forefathers whose wisdom they refresh to our ears—summon us to strenuous faithfulness as stewards of God's mysteries, men shaped by Christ and his cross, bringing God's message of astonishing grace, into a milieu in need of the hope that only the Sovereign Creator-Redeemer can give."

—DENNIS E. JOHNSON, Professor Emeritus of Practical Theology, Westminster Seminary California

"These three essays by esteemed pastor-theologians give us much food for thought concerning a mind that discerns the secularizing trends of our culture, a heart inflamed with love for God and people, and a life of caring sacrificially for Christ's flock. A much-needed book abounding with valuable insights for pastors and ministry for a very needy day and a very secular world!"

—JOEL R. BEEKE, President, Puritan Reformed Theological Seminary, Grand Rapids, Michigan

"In 1969, Martyn Lloyd-Jones gave a series of lectures on preaching at WTS in which he answered the question, 'What is preaching?' with the now iconic answer: 'Logic on fire.' He taught, 'Light without heat never affected anybody. Heat without light is no good. You must have light and heat.' The Boyer Lectures from William Edgar, Kent Hughes, and Alfred Poirier provide the preacher plenty of light and heat! Edgar's 'Are We Really Secular?' masterfully explores—in the Bible and throughout culture—that question and offers a Scriptural solution to secularization. Hughes's 'The Heart of the Pastor and the Pulpit' offers insights and inspired reflections on preaching Christ from our hearts to the hearts of our people. Poirier's 'Gregory of Nazianzus and the Pastor as the Physician of Souls' looks back in history to Gregory's struggles and offers lessons learned that will lift our eyes to Christ and encourage us to put our hands to the plow of pastoral ministry. So, sit down. Read through. See the light. Feel the heat. And enjoy!"

—DOUGLAS SEAN O'DONNELL, Senior Vice President of Bible Editorial, Crossway Books

"As Christians, we would never want our society to be more secular, but as Reformed Christians, we need not circle the wagons. Reformed theology has the backbone and biblical moorings for real hope, and resilient joy, in times we would not otherwise choose — even in days such as ours. These Boyer chair lectures are teeming with time-tested gold for the pastor calling to be wise as serpents with respect to our age, and innocent as doves in caring for Christ's bride. After all, it will be the 'physicians of souls' and catalysts of Christian 'affections' who, while overlooked for now, will do more to undermine Satan's schemes of inculturated unbelief. And one day soon they will be vindicated, and cherished."

—DAVID MATHIS, Senior Teacher and Executive Editor, desiringGod.org; Pastor, Cities Church, Saint Paul, Minnesota

The Pastor *and* the Modern World

# The Pastor *and* The Modern World

REFORMED MINISTRY AND SECULAR CULTURE

 WESTMINSTER SEMINARY PRESS

# Contents

# Foreword

It is my joy to introduce these lectures named for the late John Boyer—lectures which are the fruit of a very generous gift by the late Dr. John Templeton, Jr. in honor of his longtime friend and fellow elder at Proclamation Presbyterian Church, Bryn Mawr, PA.

Dr. Templeton's intent was to establish a permanent heritage to honor John Boyer's evangelistic concern and Christian leadership. And so, a thoroughly unique academic chair was established at Westminster, one with an explicit emphasis on personal, relevant, transformative evangelism, and its impact upon culture. Within this framework, occupants are invited to address Ethics and Apologetics, Methods of Applied Evangelism and Missions, Scholarship, and Research.

The occupant of the chair (a Westminster faculty member, visiting scholar, missionary, or evangelist) is called to aid sound, reliable, moral, and personal resilience in Christians by teaching gospel-centered biblical ethics for the Christian life. The book you hold in your hands is the culmination of those labors, a thoughtful, compelling lecture series with the purpose of evangelistic encouragement and collaboration.

I am truly grateful for these scholars' labors and for the assistance of Westminster Seminary Press in making these lovely lectures available for the first time to the public. May the passion for personal evangelism so well reflected by Mr. John Boyer's service as an elder in the church of our Lord Jesus

Christ be kindled in the hearts of many around the globe through this publication. And as Dr. Templeton intended, may our Lord be pleased to bless their message with the strengthening of his church and the advance of the gospel. Indeed, Dr. Templeton hoped that this emphasis at the seminary would motivate many to present the good news of Christ by asking, "Can I tell you what is on my heart for you?"

It was my privilege to know and to serve Christ's church with Dr. Templeton and Mr. Boyer. I am thankful that the gospel they believed and loved has now brought them to what Dr. Templeton described as "an eternity of joy" in Christ.

I would conclude with a question to the reader: "Can I tell you what is on my heart for you?" It is this:

> If you confess with your mouth that Jesus is Lord and believe in your heart that God raised him from the dead, you will be saved. For with the heart one believes and is justified, and with the mouth one confesses and is saved. For the Scripture says, "Everyone who believes in him will not be put to shame." For there is no distinction between Jew and Greek, for the same Lord is Lord of all, bestowing his riches on all who call on him. For "everyone who calls on the name of the Lord will be saved" (Rom. 10:9–13).

Sincerely in Christ's service,

Peter A. Lillback
President, Westminster Theological Seminary
Winter 2020

*Peter A. Lillback (left) with the first three occupants of the Boyer Chair: William Edgar (center left), R. Kent Hughes (center right), and Alfred Poirier (right)*

# A Note on the Text
# and Acknowledgments

The lectures included in this book were delivered in the order they are presented here, in 2016, 2019, and 2021, in Rust Auditorium of Van Til Hall on the Westminster campus in Glenside, Pennsylvania. Each has been tailored from its original oral presentation to better suit book form, but their substance has not been significantly altered.

The original intent was to publish each lecture on its own as a pamphlet. Providentially, however, the lectures only became ready for publication after the delivery of the third lecture in 2021. With all three in hand, their thematic sequence presented a cohesive collection that could serve the church, and especially the ministers of the church, with illuminating insight into the relationship of the pastor to the world that could be digested in a weekend's reading. In light of this, it seemed more than natural that William Edgar's brilliant modern cultural analysis should be paired with R. Kent Hughes's loupe-like study of the timeless essentials of pastoral ministry, and that the conclusion should be a vision for ministry that Alfred Poirier mined from the ancient life of Gregory of Nazianzus. Although each author wrote in his own distinct style—Edgar in sophisticated prose, Hughes methodical and precise, and Poirier in warm, conversational tones—it seemed best that the three be made available as one, so as not to deprive the benefit of one from the other.

Thanks are due to Randall Pederson, Pierce T. Hibbs, and Rachel Stout for their excellent editorial work in helping to gently shape these lectures into book form. Josiah Pettit, Director of Publishing at WSP, and Kyle Whitgrove, Operations Manager, both contributed to the shape of the book. Victor Kim took the photograph on page xiii.

This project would not have been possible without the leadership of WSP's board of managers: Peter A. Lillback, David B. Garner, Chun Lai, Lee Augsburger, and Jim Sweet. K. Scott Oliphint, John Currie, and Todd M. Rester all very generously contributed thoughtful introductions to the lectures. Finally, we wish to thank the authors of this book—William Edgar, R. Kent Hughes, and Alfred Poirier—for their patience, and especially for their living practice of wholehearted commitment to the Savior they preach.

Westminster Seminary Press
Spring 2022

The Pastor *and* the Modern World

# Are We Really Secular?

William Edgar

# Introduction

It is an honor to have the opportunity to introduce my mentor and colleague, Dr. William Edgar, to the readers of this lecture. One often hears that "this man needs no introduction." Dr. Edgar is the only person I've ever met of whom, no matter the venue, it can accurately be said that "this man needs no introduction." His influence and reputation extend, literally, around the world. There is hardly a place on the globe where Dr. Edgar and his wife, Barbara, are strangers.

Readers of this penetrating lecture have the opportunity to witness the work of a theologian who possesses the unique ability to understand a wide range of disciplines, and to interact with them in a way that glorifies our Savior. In this sense, Dr. Edgar is one of very few Renaissance men left.

For example, I know of no biblically and theologically grounded apologists who deal with topics such as beauty in the way that Dr. Edgar does. In his article, "Beauty Avenged, Apologetics Enriched," he says:

> There is a reality to beauty because there is a transcendental ground which gives everything, including the aesthetic, meaning. The Creator, redeemer God, the covenant Lord who makes and remakes a world of meaning, is the all-sufficient warrant for truth. The artistic endeavor is one of many proofs for the

wisdom of God. What could be more appropriate to persuade a lost generation about the love and justice of God than the wise appropriation of artistic examples and gifts that articulate the true story of the gospel in a way that speaks to the soul? What could be more apt to denounce idols, which always distort beauty by either degrading it or deifying it, than an apologetic enriched by a biblically-based aesthetic? What more important approach to the transformation of culture could there be than articulating a Christian worldview in which aesthetics occupies its rightful place?[1]

It would be difficult to find another Reformed apologist who is able to synthesize these ideas into such a singular contribution to the discipline of apologetics and to the church. Because of his gifts and background, Dr. Edgar is uniquely qualified to help us navigate the differences and affinities between two of his revered mentors, Francis Schaeffer and Cornelius Van Til. His assessment of both men, in his 1995 article on "Two Christian Warriors: Cornelius Van Til and Francis A. Schaeffer Compared,"[2] is the definitive statement, even beyond what Van Til himself wrote, on how best to understand the respective strengths and weaknesses of these two devoted apologists.

More than twenty years ago, in his prescient and penetrating article on postmodernism, Dr. Edgar was able to see and dig up the roots of the problem of the postmodern, while

1. William Edgar, "Beauty Avenged, Apologetics Enriched." *Westminster Theological Journal* 63, no. 1 (Spring 2001): 107–22.

2. William Edgar, "Two Christian Warriors: Cornelius Van Til and Francis A. Schaeffer Compared," *Westminster Theological Journal* 57, no. 1 (Spring 1995): 57–80.

others were either adopting it or simply skimming the surface. In "No News is Good News: Modernity, The Postmodern, and Apologetics," he says:

> Even the most radical and skeptical postmodernists find themselves un-consciously appealing to the very standards they reject. Christopher Norris has shown how a scholar like Stanley Fish, in his vehement attacks on theory as a mere justification of personal preference, perpetuates the illusion that he is somehow outside of the confines of that personal preference. The reason-freedom dialectic cannot be left off unless a deeper challenge is made. Again, this is where a transcendental approach is able to clear away the underbrush. Because God is fully rational, and because human knowledge is revelatory of that God, dependent rather than independent, our knowledge has meaning, and we can properly understand the world without falling into a dialectical labyrinth.[3]

Here Dr. Edgar sifts through the clouds of confusion to affirm that our grasp of God's world is possible only because of who God is. This truth dissolves the challenges of postmodern relativism, and of any other view that tries to suppress the reality of God's existence and presence.

But Dr. Edgar does not confine himself to the classroom. He has the enviable ability to move from the classroom to the living room, from the academy to the couch. In his

---

3. William Edgar, "No News is Good News: Modernity, The Postmodern, and Apologetics," *Westminster Theological Journal* 57, no. 2 (Fall 1995): 359–82.

profound book, *The Face of Truth*,[4] he shows, at a popular level, how skepticism and so many other attempts to avoid God are rooted in decisions to avoid reality as it is given by God in his world. Not only this, but in his book for young adults, *You Asked*,[5] he even bothers to answer a question readers will be hard pressed to find in any other book on apologetics: "Are there Vampires?"

Dr. Edgar was kind enough, at its release, to give me a signed copy of what is now my favorite of his books, *Schaeffer on the Christian Life*.[6] I read most of the book in one sitting. In it, Dr. Edgar reminded me of what Schaeffer called "The Final Apologetic." For Schaeffer, the final apologetic, the climactic defense of Christianity, was to be found in the love that true Christians show toward one another. Dr. Edgar has, as an example to so many of us, lived that final apologetic in a way that few have done.

After this lecture is read, it would benefit the reader to take advantage of the other writings of Dr. Edgar. Whether your interest is in theology, apologetics, art, music, jazz, or medical ethics, you will find insights that I have found nowhere else. So, *tolle lege*—take and read—enjoy, and then pick up another work from Dr. Edgar and continue to read.

K. Scott Oliphint
Fall 2019

4. William Edgar, *The Face of Truth: Lifting the Veil* (Phillipsburg, NJ: P&R, 2001).

5. William Edgar, *You Asked: Your Questions. God's Answers* (Geanies House: Christian Focus Publications, 2013).

6. William Edgar, *Schaeffer on the Christian Life: Countercultural Spirituality* (Wheaton, IL: Crossway, 2013).

# Are We Really Secular?

In 2014, Alain de Botton, along with John Armstrong, sponsored an important art exhibit at Amsterdam's museum of modern art, the Rijksmuseum. The title of the exhibit was *Art Is Therapy*. Their book, *Art as Therapy*, makes the argument for the show, and for their overall philosophy that the museum has replaced the church in today's culture.[1]

In times past, one would have entered a church to confess sins and find absolution. But today the church is gone, and standing in its place is the art museum, where viewers can happily attend, and find the same kind of spiritual help they used to find in the church. Viewers may find in the exhibit themes such as "love & relationships, work, status, memory and mortality." Consequently, prints on the themes of "Fortune, Politics, Sex and Money" were featured, using the extensive Rijksmuseum's collection from the period 1485–1800.

It would be hard to find a more apt metaphor to describe the titanic shift in the history of ideas labeled "secularization." What stands out is the way the big questions, such as love, God, and forgiveness, have not been so much marginalized,

1. See Alain de Botton and John Armstrong, *Art as Therapy* (London and New York: Phaidon Press, 2013). I am grateful to Robb Ludwick at Dutch l'Abri for introducing me to these theories.

let alone disparaged, as they have been recast and redefined. Traditional secularization theory once predicted the demise of religion. We now realize that is an impossibility.

Terry Eagleton described the phenomenon this way: "Not believing in God is a far more arduous affair than is generally imagined. Whenever the Almighty seems safely dispatched, he is always liable to stage a reappearance in one disguise or another."[2]

The quote lacks reverence. But Eagleton has captured something of crucial importance for evangelism and culture. In these few pages, I would like to explore the way historians and sociologists have predicted God's disappearance, and how they have got it wrong; at least we thought they did.

## The Journey toward the Self

What exactly is secularization? It is not an abstract concept. In fact, it can be measured, and even felt. Think along the lines of De Botton's and Armstrong's assumption: church attendance in the West is in a free fall, God is increasingly absent in cultural documents and instruments, and our laws are less and less informed by theological principles.

Michel Vovelle's study of the shift in the language of last wills and testaments over the centuries is revealing. Whereas in premodern times people were likely to require a priest by their deathbeds and to leave money to the church, Vovelle discovered that, as modernity advanced, this language was increasingly modified so as to leave out the rite of Extreme

2. Terry Eagleton, *Culture and the Death of God* (New Haven, CT: Yale University Press, 2014), 119.

Unction, and to bequeath assets to the family and perhaps secular charities rather than the church.[3]

Secularization can also be felt in daily life. A strong push for self-reliance has replaced trusting in God. Consider a television commercial for the drug dulaglutide (Trulicity). It's a drug meant to combat diabetes. This ad, along with others related to health products, tends to appear on programs watched by older persons. What is striking about this particular ad is its perfect accord with modern individualism. An attractive, well-preserved older person is pictured along with the caption: "By activating what's within me."

Then come the requisite two minutes of disclaimers. The warnings go something like this: "Don't use it if you have multiple endocrine neoplasia syndrome type 2 (MEN 2), or a personal or family history of medullary thyroid carcinoma (a type of thyroid cancer). Do not use Trulicity if you are in a state of diabetic ketoacidosis." Perhaps the most (unintentionally) amusing is, "Don't use dulaglutide if you're allergic to dulaglutide." Such warnings are extensive, often recycling language such as "Tell your doctor if…" Presumably this is to avoid lawsuits. The Trulicity ad goes on to tell you the answers for your problem are *within you*. Taking the drug is to "Click to Activate Your Within."

But aren't medicines meant to *combat* something wrong inside you? Of course, but that isn't the message of this commercial. It may be true that good medicines work with your body, but the suggestion here is that all the good stuff is already there inside you. You already have what it takes. You're just a click away from releasing the goodness. In this pharmaceutical

3. Michel Vovelle, *Piété baroque et déchristianisation en Provence au xviiie siècle. Les attitudes devant la mort d'après les clauses de testaments* (Paris: Seuil, 1973).

commercial we see a vivid illustration of a major feature of secularization: the shift from the objective to the subjective.

Illustrations of this shift abound. A similar emphasis on the subjective is commonly heard in public speeches. Recently, I've attended a good many graduation ceremonies. Most of us do not pay much attention to graduation speeches. The graduates certainly don't! But lately I've tried to listen. Almost uniformly, even in the Christian school our grandchildren attend, the messages have applied a slightly more poetic rendering of "Click to Activate Your Within."

Here's a sampling from an online collection:[4]

"You have to leave the city of your comfort and go into the wilderness of your intuition. You can't get there by bus, only by hard work and risk and by not quite knowing what you're doing, but what you'll discover will be wonderful. What you'll discover will be yourself." (Alan Alda)

Notice the romantic contrast between the city and the wilderness, almost as if we are going on a holiday to get away from it all, only to arrive at…the self.

"Have the courage to follow your heart and intuition. They somehow already know what you truly want to become. Everything else is secondary." (Steve Jobs)

"You can Google for an answer. You can Google for a mate. You can Google for a career. But you can't Google to find what's in your heart—the passion that lifts you skyward." (Joe Plumeri)

This sort of oratory has become so familiar we hardly recognize the remarkable, though subtle, history behind it. The turn of our focus away from the transcendent and toward the immanent did not occur recently or suddenly. How did we develop such a mentality? A number of scholars propose

4. There are any number of sites carrying such quotes. These ones are from http://www.graduationwisdom.com/quotes/01-life-rules-from-graduation-speeches-find-your-passion.html.

understanding secularization as a shift from a world organized by a more unified, theocentric principle to one of *social differentiation*.[5] By this they mean that whereas the church once was the integration point for all of life, it is now only one part of many this-worldly domains. The church has been uncoupled from the state, and the family. Religion has been made into a private affair. It may still be a guiding myth for some, but it is no longer obligatory, exclusive truth.[6]

## The Mechanics of Secularization

The word *secularization* is a loaded term that has served many purposes, but if we follow the categories carefully set forth by scholar C. John Sommerville, we may identify at least six concrete usages: (1) It can mean social differentiation, as we have seen. (2) It can refer to the drift of institutions, such as universities, from their original religious purpose to something far broader.[7] (3) It can mean the transfer of certain activities from the church to the government, as seen in the shift in financial support for humanitarian relief organizations from the church to the state. (4) It can refer to this-worldly lifestyles, or

5. See, for example, José Casanova, "Rethinking Secularization: A Global Comparative Perspective," The Hedgehog Review (Spring/Summer 2006): 7–22.

6. See Fojio Ikado, "The Search for a Definition of Secularization: Toward a General Theory," https://www2.kokugakuin.ac.jp/ijcc/wp/cimac/ikado.html.

7. C. J. Sommerville, "Secular Society/Religious Population: Our Tacit Rules for Using the Term 'Secularization,'" Journal for the Scientific Study of Religion 37, no. 2 (June 1998): 249–53. Somerville cites Harvard University as an example. Originally founded to train ministers, its motto was Veritas Christo et Ecclesia (Truth for Christ and the Church). Now a highly pluralistic center of learning, Harvard's motto has been reduced to simply Veritas.

a mentality that understands issues in light of the present order, rather than the life to come. (5) It generally describes the decline of religious practice in a people group or population, rather than an individual. (6) And it identifies *religion* in its broadest sense, rather than, say, the Christian faith or a particular denomination.[8]

In view of so many applications of the same term, some specialists abandon the word altogether. Yet I think there are compelling reasons to keep it, so long as we take care not to use it cheaply, as an indolent way to signify any social condition one isn't happy with.[9] As British sociologist David Lyon argues, "Contemporary cultural analysis cannot dispense with some reference to 'secularization,' any more than general historical sociology can. That—not to mention its decisive impact on Christian practice—is why it is important."[10] Lyon goes on to suggest that secularization is a mode, or, as he puts it, a "problematic." This may sound like academic jargon, but the term simply refers to a complex set of forces, which together make up the reality of secularization.

In order to investigate such a problematic and to arrive at an understanding of the surrounding world, let us briefly survey three crucial steps: first, a short presentation of the standard or classical secularization thesis; second, the recognition of its severe limits; third, revisiting the thesis with nuance and amplification. Then it will be possible to post some responses and suggest action points for the church.

---

8. Sommerville, "Secular Society/Religious Population," 249–53.

9. This is the case with expressions such as "secular humanism."

10. David Lyon, *The Steeple's Shadow: On the Myths and Realities of Secularization* (London: SPCK, 1985), 22. Karel Dobbelaere argues similarly for a multi-facetted usage. See his *Secularization: An Analysis at Three Levels* (Brussels: Presses Interuniversitaires Européennes, 2004), 25.

## The Standard Model

When most people think of secularization, they think of what we may call the standard model. Bryan Wilson's simple definition is perhaps most useful, "[Secularization] maintains no more than that religion ceases to be significant in the working of the social system"[11]

The same idea can be expressed prescriptively rather than descriptively. As "new atheist" Richard Dawkins puts it, "Many of us saw religion as harmless nonsense. Beliefs might lack all supporting evidence but, we thought, if people needed a crutch for consolation, where's the harm? September 11th changed all that."[12] For Dawkins, religion is so much harmless nonsense until it shows its true colors, the unleashing of violence in its name. Unlike Wilson, Dawkins believes religion is significant, but only in a negative sense.

A slightly more technical way of expressing the standard model recognizes the way secularization spreads into various sectors of social and intellectual life. This approach focuses on the way differentiation actually grows. Still following Wilson, we are dealing with "the societalization of subsystems in the organized world."[13] To express the standard model more simply, we can go

11. Bryan R. Wilson, *Religion in Sociological Perspective* (New York: Oxford University Press, 1982), 150.

12. *The Guardian* (UK edition), October 11, 2001.

13. Subsystems are also *gesellschaftlich*, or societalized. The organized world is "based on impersonal roles, relationships, the coordination of skills, and essentially formal and contractual patterns of behavior, in which personal virtue, as distinguished from role obligations, is of small consequence" (Wilson, *Religion in Sociological Perspective*, 155). In such systems, Wilson goes on, control is no longer based on morals and religion; it has become impersonal, a matter of routine techniques and unknown officials—legal, technical, mechanized, computerized, and electronic. Thus religion has lost one of its important latent functions; as long as control

back to Sommerville and note that "Secularization [means] a significant *shift in attention* from ultimate 'religious' concerns to proximate concerns."[14] This shift is a process over time.

## Origins of the Standard Model

It is fair to say that by the 1960s some variety of this view was held by a majority of sociologists. And it came with a pedigree. The view was tethered to the long history of the evolutionary idea that humanity would outgrow the need for religion, an idea with clear roots in the Enlightenment idea that the world, including people, is governed by laws, and that these laws may be accessed through unaided reason. Says Stewart Brown, "[The Enlightenment] was ordered by a common project: the belief that the universe was governed by constant and uniform laws, and that through reason – the objective, critical and logical processes of the human mind – humankind could achieve knowledge of those universal laws."[15]

By implication, the claims of revealed religion are obviated in such a world, or at least marginalized. Again, there was prescriptive doctrine. Stark and Bainbridge put it this way: "At least since the Enlightenment, most Western intellectuals have anticipated the death of religion . . ." They add that "The most illustrious figures in sociology, anthropology, and psychology

---

was interpersonal, it was based on religiously based mores and substantive values.

14. Sommerville, "Secular Society/Religious Population," 249.

15. Stewart J. Brown, "Religion and the Enlightenment," *Enlightenment and Secularization: Course of Modernization in Both the West and the East* (Wuhan University, 2006), 1. See also *The Cambridge History of Christianity: Enlightenment, Reawakening and Revolution, 1660-1815*, vol. 7, eds, Stewart J. Brown and Timothy Tackett (Cambridge: Cambridge University Press, 2007).

have unanimously expressed confidence that their children, or surely their grandchildren, would live to see the dawn of a new era in which, to paraphrase Freud, the infantile illusions of religion would be outgrown."[16]

No doubt these Enlightenment principles found their most radical expression in France. Speaking of religion, the notorious pundit Voltaire is said to have expostulated, "Écrasez l'infâme" (crush the infamous thing). His lifelong enemies were Jansenism, Calvinism, and especially the Roman Catholic Church. What Voltaire was really against was any ideology that appeared to be intolerant.

Very few of the Enlightenment thinkers would compromise with the traditional view, but Voltaire worried that if his words were taken literally, it would incite murder. Thus, his famous phrase, "If God did not exist, we would have to invent him." Religion, he said, was fine, as long as it was what he called the pure religion of a human Jesus. Significantly, in *Candide* (1759), his devastating critique of Leibnizian Christianity, or *optimism*, his young ("candid") adventurer, after enduring scores of calamities, asks Master Pangloss (who is Leibniz) why this has to be. And each time, the answer comes, it is the *best of all possible worlds*; the evil is necessary for the greater good. After trying to see a silver lining everywhere, exhausted, Candide comes back to the only remaining task: cultivation of his garden, a clear allusion to Eden. Here even Voltaire acknowledged something of mankind's beginnings and the need to somehow reset in a biblical way.

In fact, the Enlightenment story was never a rejection of religion pure and simple, contrary to Bainbridge and Stark's claims. There were attempts in various ways and in various

16. Rodney Stark and William Sims Bainbridge, *The Future of Religion: Secularization, Revival, and Cult Formation* (Berkeley: University of California Press, 1985), 1.

countries to effect a happy marriage between its rationalism and the Christian religion. The result was often a reduction of the Christian faith to deism. Book titles such as John Toland's give us an idea: *Christianity Not Mysterious*.[17] Still, with just a little help from revelation, the achievement of the knowledge of the laws of the cosmos was agreed to be within reach.

## Max Weber

At a more analytical level, the remarkable sociologist and philosopher Max Weber (1864–1920) has explained how secularization not only means the decline of religion, but the insertion of three basic values: intellectualization, rationalization, and disenchantment.

By *intellectualization*, Weber did not mean we are getting smarter, even though we are becoming more and more specialized. He meant that there are fewer and fewer incalculable forces. Yet, the consequence is not a healthy sense of mystery. The end result, as Tolstoy taught him, is a meaningless universe. The elevation of science means that thoughtful action is being replaced by an endless quest for experience.[18]

*Rationalization* is central to Weber's understanding of secularization. One of the most famous images conveying his view is "the iron cage."

The iron cage is actually a translation by sociologist Talcott Parsons of Weber's view of reason, which is "a shell as

17. Published in 1697, it was meant to be an apologetic for an enlightened faith. Condemned by the church at first, it soon became widely available.

18. See Peter Lassman and Irving Velody, with Herminio Martins, eds., *Max Weber's 'Science as a Vocation'* (New York: Routledge, 1989).

hard as steel."[19] The idea is that modern society is developing with more and more bureaucracy, the influence of which is felt in every sphere of society, from law to economics to education. The result, he argued, was that the rationalized society was crowding out human experience, so that people were becoming alienated. Weber had read Tolstoy and was influenced by his image of the impersonal machine of modernity. Tolstoy wrote some of his major works shortly after the abolition of serfdom in 1861, a time that saw Russia becoming increasingly bureaucratic. Toward the end of his monumental *War and Peace,* a character named Pierre is imprisoned. In his incarceration, Pierre begins to feel the oppression of a larger system. The author remarks, "A system of some sort was killing him – Pierre – depriving him of life, of everything, annihilating him… [Pierre is a] small cog in a ceaselessly moving mechanism."[20]

For Weber, rationality in modern times replaces tradition, emotion, and personality. Following Weber, French sociologist Jacques Ellul considers technology (or "technique" as he prefers to call it) to be the major scourge of our times. Modern science, he says, fathered modern technology, which is a predator. He puts it this way: "Modern technology has become a total phenomenon for civilization, the defining force of a new social order in which efficiency is no longer an option but a necessity imposed on all human activity."[21]

19. The image occurs toward the end of Weber's *The Protestant Ethic and the Spirit of Capitalism* (1905, 1958). See Edward Tyryakian, "The Sociological Import of a Metaphor: Tracking the Source of Max Weber's Iron Cage," *Sociological Inquiry* 51, no. 1 (January 1981): 27–33.

20. Quoted in Jeremy Klemin, "Behind the Iron Cage: What Can Max Weber Tell Us about Leo Tolstoy?" http://www.3ammagazine.com/3am/behind-the-iron-cage-what-can-max-weber-tell-us-about-leo-tolstoy.

21. Jacques Ellul, *The Technological System*, trans. Joachim Neugroschel (New York: Continuum, 1980), 21.

Finally, Weber's *disenchantment* is a historical process whereby everything in life is understood as being less mysterious, and more knowable by human rationality. Here is where secularization occurs in its full force. Weber did not think, as did Nietzsche, that God was gone. But he thought there was less hope to be had through faith.

We can see how the three ideas (intellectualization, rationalization, and disenchantment) are interconnected. Weber argued that the three arose because of the Reformation's house-cleaning. That is, Protestants had swept away demons and spirits and left a great deal of room for hard work, untethered by norms from above. Although Protestants from Calvin to Wesley warned against the abuses of prosperity, their focus on discipline and hard work paved the way to a free market.[22]

One popular corollary to Weber's view is the so-called "gravedigger theory." What the theory argues is that the Protestant church, having gradually cleared out many aspects of a supernatural universe, generated inertia that eventually caused the "burial" of God himself. This might well have had the effect of disillusioning people. Weber himself was unhappy about these developments. Attempts at making the best of it came from different places. Riffing off Weber's concept, for example, Jean-Paul Sartre once said that any dreamer who sees the world in an enchanted way, seeing the good everywhere, is going to confront the truth

22. In reality, the Weber Thesis has been oversimplified. Weber's original idea was that Protestantism was rather an ascetic religion. It morphed into a "spirit" of hard work, leading to a lifestyle of hard work. This in turn could lead to market capitalism, but not necessarily. Subsequent commentators often simplified the thesis into saying God's people may have assurance of their divine election by the wealth they have accumulated, which is simply not what Weber taught.

and experience a major disillusion. Yet, one may refuse to cave-in to pessimism, he explained, by an existentialist leap of faith. The mistake, according to Sartre, is to stop at such disillusion, and forbid any reasons for moving on.

## Within Christendom

According to the standard model, secularization can be detected in every domain. We tend to think of it happening outside of the church, or outside of Christian endeavors, but of course Christendom is not exempt. Even biblical studies can be secularized. The rise of biblical criticism exhibits this gradual incursion of secularization. As Michael C. Legaspi points out, the spirit of the Enlightenment gradually transformed the Bible from a sacred book to a text to be studied. In his examination of the work of little-known biblical scholar Johann David Michaelis (1717–91), Legaspi argues that, "The academic Bible was created by scholars who saw that the scriptural Bible, embedded as it was in confessional particularities, was inimical to the socio-political project from which Enlightenment universities draw their purpose and support." Legaspi's view focuses on "social causes" rather than "intellectual antinomies" such as the tension between faith and reason.[23]

An obvious measure of secularization in the church is the decline in attendance. This is perhaps the most dramatic measure warranting the standard model.

23. Michael Legaspi, *The Death of Scripture and the Rise of Biblical Studies* (New York: Oxford University Press, 2010), viii–ix. See Daniel Timmer's review of Legaspi's book in *Themelios* 36, no. 1 (April 2011): 60–61, http://themelios.thegospelcoalition.org/review/the-death-of-scripture-and-the-rise-of-biblical-studies.

Years ago, I taught at a seminary in Quebec. For convenience, it met in a large church in downtown Montreal. Known as Erskine and American, as the name suggests, the church has its roots in a merger between two denominations, both going back to 1823. The building's architect was the well-known church designer, H. C. Hutchison. The interior is rich with wooden pews, and there are impressive stained-glass windows, including a number by L. C. Tiffany. By the twenty-first century, numbers were dwindling, and the church could no longer sustain the cost of its existence. So, the building was sold in 2007 to the art museum across the way. Today, Erskine and American is a pavilion of the *Musée des beaux-arts*. The exhibits are mostly from the history of Canadian art, including Inuit works. So, there you have it: what used to be an active church is now a museum.

Statistics for the decline in church attendance are somewhat hard to come by. But, such as they are, they may help. The decline is more pronounced in Europe than elsewhere. And even there it varies by country. The Church of England (the established church, but hardly the only one) closes about twenty churches per year. In Denmark, some two hundred churches have either been closed or deemed unusable. In Germany, the Roman Catholic churches have closed over five hundred churches in the last decade. Perhaps the most dramatic figures come from the Netherlands. There over one thousand Roman Catholic churches and seven hundred Protestant churches that will soon close.

What is striking is to see how the old church buildings are repurposed. There is the call to therapy at the Rijksmuseum, and there is the art museum in Montreal, just mentioned. In the Soviet Union, one thinks of the beautiful "Moscow Baroque" Novodevichy Convent, whose bells used to ring for vespers to the surrounding population. In 1922, the Bolsheviks turned the place into a museum of female emancipation. Of course, they were "emancipated into factories and collective farms."[24] In Holland, it is not uncommon for church buildings to be turned into a supermarket, a bookstore, even a gymnasium. In England, there is a considerable push to sell old churches in order to make them into people's homes.[25]

The story in the United States is a bit different. Americans are generally more observant than Europeans, and so the numbers are not quite so dramatic. Surveys such as those conducted by the Gallup organization show Americans attending church at a rate of about 40%. Yet, a few qualifications mitigate what otherwise would be an impressive statistic. For example, while a good number of Protestants identify with "the church," they do not necessarily attend church all that regularly, nor do many of them even belong to

24. As Peter Hitchens points out in, "The Cold War Is Over," *First Things* (October 2016), 35. This kind of transformation happened regularly in the former Soviet Union. Hundreds of churches were turned into museums. During the 1930s the number of Orthodox churches in Russia dropped from nearly 30,000 down to 500. See Dimitry V. Pospielovsky, *The Russian Church Under the Soviet Regime, 1917–1982* (Yonkers, NY: St. Vladimir's Seminary Press, 1984).

25. See Naftali Bendavid, "Europe's Empty Churches Go on Sale," *The Wall Street Journal* (Jan. 2), 2015, http://www.wsj.com/articles/europes-empty-churches-go-on-sale-1420245359. For details regarding this decline, consider church attendance per percentage of the population in the following countries:

| Denmark | 3% |
| Sweden | 5% |
| Finland | 5% |
| France | 12% |
| Great Britain | 12% |
| United States | 39% |

https://en.wikipedia.org/wiki/Religion_in_Europe.

a particular church.[26] Even the megachurches, so characteristic of American religion, are experiencing a decline.[27] Added to this is the question of what kind of Christian faith Americans actually believe. For example, about 52% of Americans believe Jesus was human and committed sins like anyone else.[28] Only 26% of Americans believe sin makes God angry.[29]

## But Is It So Simple?

Inevitable decline? Wait just a moment! Something rather surprising has happened. For many reasons, the standard model has come under scrutiny. As it happens, many sociologists, even strong advocates for the standard model of secularization, have reversed themselves.

One example of such a *volte-face*, a most significant one, is that of Peter L. Berger. Bluntly, as he puts it in an interview:

> I think what I and most other sociologists of religion wrote in the 1960s about secularization was a mistake. Our underlying argument was that secularization and modernity go hand in hand. With more modernization comes more secularization. It

26. See Kelly Shattuck, "Seven Startling Facts: An Up Close Look at Church Attendance in America," *Church Leaders* (Dec. 29, 2015), http://churchleaders.com/pastors/pastor-articles/139575-7-startling-facts-an-up-close-look-at-church-attendance-in-america.html.

27. See Samuel Smith, "Megachurches Seeing Drop in Weekly Attendance, Study Finds," http://www.christianpost.com/news/megachurches-growing-face-declining-weekly-attendance-protestant-church-151570.

28. Harris Poll (April 1, 2015), https://www.barna.com/research/what-do-americans-believe-about-jesus-5-popular-beliefs/#.

29. Rodney Stark, *What Americans Really Believe* (Waco, TX: Baylor University Press, 2008), 76.

wasn't a crazy theory. There was some evidence for it. But I think it's basically wrong. Most of the world today is certainly not secular. It's very religious. So is the U.S. The one exception to this is Western Europe. One of the most interesting questions in the sociology of religion today is not, How do you explain fundamentalism in Iran? but, Why is Western Europe different?[30]

What had been the methodological error? Berger had wrongly linked various features of modernity with inevitable secularization.

The mistake, I think, can be described as a confusion of categories: Modernity is not necessarily secularizing; it is necessarily *pluralizing*. Modernity is characterized by an increasing plurality, within the same society, of different beliefs, values, and worldviews. Plurality does indeed pose a challenge to all religious traditions: each one must cope with the fact that there are 'all these others,' not just in a faraway country but right next door. This challenge, however, is *not* the one assumed by secularization theory.[31]

30. "Epistemological Modesty: An Interview with Peter Berger," *The Christian Century* (October 29, 1997), 972–78, https://www.religion-online.org/article/epistemological-modesty-an-interview-with-peter-berger/.

31. Peter L. Berger, "Secularization Falsified," *First Things* (February 2008), https://www.firstthings.com/article/2008/02/002-secularization-falsified.

Typically comical about how such an error can be made, Berger describes receiving the first volume of the heavily funded *Fundamentalism Project*. It led him to an "aha" moment. Why would North American academics be interested in fundamentalism, he wondered? First, he says, peevishly, it's a matter of knowing your enemy! But second, it was such a puzzle to these close-minded scholars that so many people passionately believed something; it needed figuring out. He realized that in fact the real puzzle is these North American academics, who seemed to live in a cocoon. That might be worth a heavily funded study![32]

Berger's revolution was accompanied by a good deal of research on the presence of religion throughout the world. Often it is couched as a resurgence. Roman Catholic scholars such as Philip Jenkins and Rodney Stark have led the charge.[33] Philip Jenkins initiated a series of studies that have characterized his career with *The Next Christendom*, an extensive study of church growth in the Southern Hemisphere.[34] Jenkins believes Westerners have been looking in the wrong places for their evaluation of the health of the modern church. Like Berger's interlocutors, they have been lamenting the slow decline of the church because their vision is limited to a liberal, Westernized version of the manifestation of Christianity. Rather, if we acknowledged the conservative character of worldwide faith,

32. Peter L. Berger, "The Desecularization of the World: A Global Overview," in ed. Peter L. Berger, *The Desecularization of the Word: Resurgent Religion and World Politics* (Washington, DC: Ethics and Public Policy Center; Grand Rapids: Eerdmans, 1999), 2.

33. Peter Berger was a Protestant. Often Roman Catholics show a greater interest in earthly manifestations of heavenly matters. Perhaps this owes something to the Thomist tradition of natural theology.

34. Philip Jenkins, *The Next Christendom: The Coming of Global Christianity* (New York: Oxford University Press, 2002).

we would observe a great resurgence, even an explosion of the church in places such as Sub-Saharan Africa, Latin America, and South Asia. In this and in later studies Jenkins notes the seriousness with which the Southern Hemisphere church takes the Bible, as well as the role of prayer and a recognition of the reality of the supernatural, including angels and demons.[35]

The Christian faith is not the only growing religious movement to be observed. My family and I were living in Europe when the Iranian Revolution occurred (February through December 1979). Within a few months, the country moved from something like an emerging democracy under Reza Shah Pahlavi to the clerical government of the Ayatollah Khomeini. Americans, as well as Europeans, were caught off guard. Many of the editorials in the local newspapers, as well as the *New York Times* expressed dismay and surprise that a country moving toward modernization, with its different rights and freedoms, could suddenly want to go "backwards." Notice the lingering historiography of progress, the dominant view held in the Enlightenment. Today we have come a long way in understanding the rise of Islamic states, but we still have difficulty fitting it into conventional categories.[36]

## The Church and the World

While many religions are growing, the resiliency of the Christian faith is particularly remarkable. This has been true throughout the centuries. It is particularly notable in the early

35. See particularly his *The Lost History of Christianity* (San Francisco: HarperOne, 2009), and *The New Faces of Christianity: Believing the Bible in the Global South* (New York: Oxford University Press, 2008).

36. Christians should have been the least surprised, since they understand that human beings are irrepressibly religious.

years of the church's existence in its New Testament form. Rodney Stark has focused particularly on the early church and how it rose to become the defining influence in the ancient world.[37] Among other factors contributing to the extraordinary growth of the church in the first few centuries is the emphasis on family and compassion among Christians, values less in evidence in the culture of ancient Rome. This included respect for women and the protection of infants. The Christian worldview stood in contrast to the Empire's worldly approach to power. Christians could assess the surrounding decadence and the tribulations in biblical terms. For example, they could understand the drift toward corruption as a sign of God's judgment. One compares with interest the view of Larry W. Hurtado, who builds on Stark's work and adds his own assessment of the distinctiveness of the redirected lives experienced by Christians, giving them purpose and meaning not obtainable from the surrounding culture.[38]

Many others have gotten into the act. José Casanova gained notoriety with his study of public religion.[39] What seemed to have escaped many in the West could no longer be ignored, he argues. Various events came to the attention

37. Rodney Stark, *The Rise of Christianity: How the Obscure, Marginal Jesus Movement Became the Dominant Religious Force in the Western World in a Few Centuries* (San Francisco: Harper SanFrancisco, 1997); see also his, *The Triumph of Faith: Why The World Is More Religious Than Ever* (Wilmington, DE: Intercollegiate Studies Institute, 2015). See also Mark Noll, *The New Shape of World Christianity: How American Experience Reflects Global Faith* (Downers Grove: IVP Academic, 2013).

38. Larry W. Hurtado, *Why on Earth Did Anyone Become a Christian in the First Three Centuries?* (Milwaukee: Marquette University Press, 2016); *Destroyer of the Gods: Early Christian Distinctiveness in the Roman World* (Waco: Baylor University Press, 2016).

39. José Casanova, *Public Religions in the Modern World* (Chicago: University of Chicago Press, 1994).

of the public, including, the Islamic revolution in Iran, politicized evangelical Christian support of the Reagan and Moral Majority phenomena, the first intifada in Palestine, the Sikh bodyguard assassination of Indira Gandhi, and the various religious opponents of Communism, leading to its eventual demise. Although many factors are involved, Casanova suggests one of the reasons for people to seek religious remedies for different world crises is that they cannot handle them without recourse to a higher power.[40]

A more popular way of putting this reemergence is expressed in a book by John Micklethwait and Adrian Wooldridge. They argue in *God Is Back* that whereas in Europe the Enlightenment mentality, generally suspicious of revealed religion, portrays the church as old and irrelevant, in many other parts of the world, it is quite the opposite. The book's subtitle is *How the Global Revival of Faith Is Changing the World*. Such a change, and the awareness of the change, varies a good deal from place to place. A leading government economist, Zhao Xiao, made the bold claim that there cannot be successful economic growth without a sense of "awe." His research took him to places where such growth occurred only where there were churches. In a parallel way, the host of one of the house churches in Shanghai has proclaimed that, "In Europe the church is old. Here it is modern. Religion is a sign of higher ideals and progress. Spiritual wealth and material wealth go together. That is why we will win."[41] This brother may have to learn the hard way that faith and wealth do not always go together! But what both men are arguing is

40. See Martin Riesebrodt, "Religion in the Modern World: Between Secularization and Resurgence," http://cadmus.eui.eu/bitstream/handle/1814/29698/MWP_LS_2014_01_Riesebrodt.pdf.

41. John Micklethwait and Adrian Wooldridge, *God Is Back: How the Global Revival of Faith Is Changing the World* (New York: Penguin, 2009), 9.

that higher standards of living will only occur when there is a soul, namely the church. The older communist ideology is incapable of making such a connection.

We have traveled a number of times to Wenzhou, in Zhejiang province. The city is known as one of the most prosperous in China. For various historical reasons the central government has refused to provide seed money for businesses there. That had the opposite effect from a stymie. In the absence of any constraints entrepreneurs have been quite successful. Many of them are Christians, bearing out Zhao Xiao's theory. Oddly, for China, the city boasts numerous churches, many of which are architecturally modeled after European buildings. For years, the state left the city alone since it brought economic advantages to the country. More recently, the provincial government has borne down, and destroyed a number of the churches, probably from resentment and certainly from anti-Western bias.

Clearly, then, the church appears to be in a healthy state in many parts of the world. Indeed, the growth is remarkable. In 1900, Africa had 10 million Christians representing about 10 percent of the population; by 2000, this figure had grown to 360 million, representing about half the population. Quantitatively, this may well be the largest shift in religious affiliation that has ever occurred, anywhere. In Latin America, the majority of people (some 84%) were raised in the Roman Catholic Church. Though Catholicism is declining, there is considerable growth in the Protestant churches, particularly the Pentecostal ones.[42] In Asia, it is estimated that whereas in 1990 there were 22 million Christians, today the numbers are well over 300 million.[43]

42. See the Pew Research studies at http://www.pewforum.org/2014/11/13/religion-in-latin-america.

43. A growth rate of 83%, http://www.asiaevangelicals.org/resource/churchgrowth.htm.

For Christians who believe in the Great Commission (Matt. 28:16–20), and also in our Lord's prediction that the gospel must be preached to all the nations (Matt. 24:14), such growth should not come as a surprise![44]

## Not So Fast

It appears as though everything is settled. The standard model was wrong. Religion, particularly Christianity, is exploding throughout the world, especially in the majority world. But there is still more to the story. Our third point seeks to show that along with the good news of worldwide revivals one may still diagnose traits of secularization. Indeed, on the one hand, not all the numbers point to growth, and on the other, secularization is more subtle than we might think.

To begin with there is a handful of thinkers who still think secularization is a major narrative in our times. Perhaps the most vocal is Steve Bruce. His book titles, including *God Is Dead* and *Secularization,* are eloquent. Against all the claims that religion is still vital, Bruce replies, "I am making an empirical causal claim: because privatized, compartmentalized, and individualized religion attracts less commitment, is harder to maintain, and is more difficult to pass on intact to the next generation, it fails to make up the ground lost by, and declines faster than, traditional religion…secularization is change and decline."[45]

What about the growth we have just observed in the majority world? Bruce is reserved about that as well, because,

44. Our Lord also promised the triumph of the church over the forces of hell (Matt. 16:18).

45. Steve Bruce, *Secularization; In Defense of an Unfashionable Theory* (New York: Oxford University Press, 2011), 48.

among other things, he claims it lacks depth and transformative power. Lives are not being deeply changed, nor are cultures, he argues. And when modernity comes along to many of these countries, he predicts the same thing will happen as in the West. Counter examples of religious outbreaks do not refute the thesis, since they merely slow modernization down.

Bruce is not the only skeptic. Even local leaders in those places where the growth is occurring are cautious. One Chinese pastor remarked: "Many of my people are only one unanswered prayer away from leaving the church and resorting to Buddhism or animism to solve their problems." And an African bishop recently stated: Christian faith in the Global South is "a mile wide and an inch deep."[46]

Surely, the contrarians go too far. Despite their warnings, there really are remarkable manifestations of religion around the world. The explosion of Christian faith is truly extraordinary. The warnings are sobering. There is something important to them. But credit should be given where credit is due.

But now, what I want to claim in this next portion is that secularization is still with us. It is there, alongside the growth. And it is far more pervasive, and far more subtle than is typically understood either by advocates or deniers. Secularization still envelops us like a huge wet blanket, but it emerges from surprising places. Let me outline just a few of the ways.

It is fascinating to look closely at the influential thinker who coined the term "secularization" in its modern acceptation. Auguste Comte (1798–1857), the so-called father of

---

46. Cited in Os Guinness, *Renaissance: The Power of the Gospel However Dark the Times* (Downers Grove, IL: InterVarsity Press, 2014), 36.

sociology, set forth a simple scheme. Following a common historiography, he asserted that there were three stages to human history: (1) the theological stage (with blind beliefs in the gods and magic); (2) the metaphysical stage (meaning the French philosophy of human rights, which he argued had replaced religion and blind belief); (3) the positive stage (where objective science would finally have all the answers needed to navigate the world). Comte tried to suggest the different sciences have different degrees of "positivity"—the less complex are more positive but less important. Sociology is the greatest science because it encompasses all the others.

But humankind cannot do without some object of worship. Comte proposed a new "religion of humanity" as a substitute for old superstitions. He went quite far with his view, even inventing a positivist calendar, using thirteen solar months and naming them after literary or scientific people. He wanted festival days for Catholic saints, and days of execration for people like Napoleon!

As a fascinating aside, a number of Latin American countries looked to Comte's positivism as a way to enact social reform. The greatest influence of his outlook was in Brazil, where it gained momentum in the fights against slavery, monarchy, and the Roman Catholic Church. To this day the flag of Brazil is based on Comte's view of order and progress. The motto *Ordem e Progresso* on the Brazil flag was directly inspired by his slogan, "L'amour pour principe et l'ordre pour base; le progrès pour but" (Love as a principle and order as the basis; progress as the goal).[47]

47. Raimundo Teixeiras Mendes, Brazil's president at the time, was captivated by Comte's positivism. One of the rather odd forces behind the spread of positivism in the country was the Positivist Church of Brazil, founded by Mendes's brother-in-law, Miguel Lemos. To this day there remains a Positivist Temple in Porto Alegre.

Most often, the type of standard model that predicted the demise of the church missed the presence of religion throughout the world. But some sociologists have predicted, not the absolute demise of religion, but rather a substitution, or change of location.

There is an old joke which expresses the idea. A man enters a pub in Ireland. Those at the bar ask him whether he is a Catholic or a Protestant. He assures them he is neither, that he is an atheist. "Well, are you a Catholic atheist or a Protestant atheist?" they retort.

According to these observers, the old religion (or religiosity) is alive and well, but in a different guise. Various candidates have been proposed. For example, Charles Lemert believes science has replaced religion.[48] The point is not that science has made religion obsolete, an argument that is at least as old as Marx and Freud. The point is that belief in science is itself religious in nature. For example, he suggests, the reason Émile Durkheim did not become a rabbi, as had his male ancestors for four generations, is that he found religious and moral satisfaction in modern life, which is guided by science.[49]

French historian of jurisprudence Jacques Ellul broadens out such a view by affirming the old Christian worldview has been replaced by two secular *axes* in the modern world: (1) technique and sex; (2) nation-building and revolution. These he names "the new sacred," and they occupy the same space that was once occupied by the Christian church.[50]

---

48. Charles C. Lemert, "Defining Non-Church Religion," *Review of Religions Research* 16, no. 3 (Spring 1975): 186–97.

49. Charles C. Lemert, *Sociology after the Crisis* (Boulder, CO: Paradigm, 2004), 42.

50. Jacques Ellul, *The New Demons* (New York: Seabury Press, 1975), 48–87.

Theologian Martin Marty, who is a student of religion in American history, suggests another approach. He believes modernity has seen the emergence of an autonomous, industrial culture where religion is less explicit, and yet where "salvation language" is still being used. One of his examples is the way in which John Winthrop's belief that the new world promoted a "city on a hill" had morphed into several subsequent ideologies. Manifest Destiny substituted for the Puritan mission in the nineteenth century. Ronald Reagan quoted the phrase in his farewell speech, where it signified the land of freedom and the American way.[51]

Such a view is articulated by the prolific Roman Catholic philosopher Charles Taylor. In his large tome, *A Secular Age*, he argues against the "subtraction theory" of modernity, which says that religion will simply be excluded, and for the way God is "sanctifying us everywhere," even in ordinary life.[52]

One of today's most interesting cultural critics, whom we quoted at the beginning, is Terry Eagleton. He proposes yet another candidate. Eagleton believes that culture itself has become the new religion, though he is skeptical about its chances for success. Ever since the Enlightenment, he argues, "surrogate forms of transcendence" have scrambled for the crown of the King of Kings—reason, science, literature, art, nationalism, but especially "culture"—yet none have been up to the job. Culture, he tells us, is "the most plausible candidate to inherit the scepter of religion," because it involves "foundational values,

51. Marty believes the slogan represents a widespread *Protestant* consensus that America affords a place for fresh stats, http://www.pbs.org/wnet/religionandethics/2002/05/03/may-3-2002-martin-marty-extended-interview/11648. See his "Our Religio-Secular World," *Daedalus* 132, no. 3 (Summer 2003): 42–48.

52. Charles Taylor, *A Secular Age* (Cambridge: Belknap/Harvard University Press, 2007), 326–42.

transcendent truths, authoritative traditions, ritual practices…" and much else. Yet it has been unable to do so with great success, partly because it became elitist and made some of those features unavailable to the masses.[53]

As we will see, there are good biblical reasons to observe this kind of relocation: it is at the heart of its teaching on idolatry. Almost never does the idolater tell us there is no god. Usually he says, this is what God really looks like, and proceeds to erect a counterfeit.

## Plausibility

The Christian faith is true. But then, we might ask, why don't more people believe it? Of course, the short answer is sin. We do not want to submit to God's authority. But sin is reinforced by reasons, on the one hand, but also by structures of plausibility, on the other. Something may be true but implausible. For example, you may sell the very best alpine ski equipment in the world. But to set up a shop in the Sahara Desert makes your product implausible. Or something plausible may not be true, as in the case of sin. Os Guinness, drawing on Peter Berger's work, helped Christians better to understand the role of plausibility structures for doing apologetics in *The Gravedigger File*.[54]

There has been much to make secularization plausible over the last 200 years, despite the nearly total defeat of the standard model. Owen Chadwick famously asked, what

53. Terry Eagleton, *Culture and the Death of God* (New Haven: Yale University Press, 2015), 120.

54. Os Guinness, *The Gravedigger File: Papers on the Subversion of the Modern Church* (Downers Grove: InterVarsity Press, 1983), particularly chapter 2, titled, "The Sandman Effect," putting the church to sleep about the social factors involved in belief.

happened in the twenty-five years between the publication of Darwin's *Origin of the Species* (1859) and when a young Harrow schoolboy averred that Darwin had disproved the Bible? Surely the lad did not read the book, which is daunting for anyone. Something besides the raw data (such as it was) had made the Genesis account of creation implausible.[55]

What was that something? Chadwick says it could not be the book on its own, which only sold some 1,500 copies, with many buyers expecting to find out more of the wonders of how God worked as Creator. Certain clearer scientific arguments were put forward by writers such as Owen or Huxley. Then popularizers such as Vogt or Büchner, Asa Gray and Filippo de Filippi said more and more on the area Darwin had not examined, particularly the descent of man. Then moral philosophers and theologians entered the fray. Soon, the theory became quite independent from what Darwin actually said. Indeed, there had been previous attempts to disconnect the Bible from history. "Darwin never touched the subject. But Darwin finally made it probable…"[56]

The same goes for the way much of the world embraced Marxism. Again, Chadwick says that rather than wading through the difficult texts of Marx and Engels, people felt the church was not there for them. They were hungry, and for various reasons did not trust that Christians could provide sustenance. It's a disputable claim, Chadwick argues, and yet a tenacious one. Marx did contribute to this sense

55. See Owen Chadwick, *The Secularization of the European Mind in the Nineteenth Century* (Cambridge: Cambridge University Press, 1975), 173–174.

56. Chadwick, *Secularization of the European Mind*, 174. Chadwick continues to analyze the way Darwinism spread in Germany and elsewhere. The story is similar. The particulars Darwin set forth were on the whole extraneous to the plausibility of evolution.

of implausibility. Marx ceased believing in "the gods" from 1841 onward. He gradually came to believe that religion was a major impediment to human progress. It was divisive. It was not so much that it was untrue, as that it was a moral evil. "The question is not whether religion is true or untrue, but whether it is desirable or undesirable for society."[57] Marx had more influence because of his epigrams, "opium of the people," "history repeats itself, first as tragedy, second as farce," "revolutions are the locomotives of history," and the like, than because of his economic writings. Though it is contrary to historical fact, people in the late nineteenth century felt that God was on the side of the oppressors.[58] Marxism would have no plausibility if it were not perceived as holding religious answers to the problem of alienation.

## Plausibility from the Arts

Secularization as relocation can be measured in the visual arts. A few examples from France at the turn of the twentieth century may be instructive. While a painting is not a philosophy text translated into an image, it does nevertheless articulate a worldview. We can learn much about the dynamics of culture from an understanding of the significant pictures from a particular period.

It was a time of extraordinary change. Robert Hughes helps us understand the way modern art greeted modernity. He quotes Charles Péguy, who was one of the most thoughtful writers and social critics of the early twentieth century. In 1913, he said this: "the world has changed less since the

57. Chadwick, *Secularization of the European Mind*, 59.
58. Chadwick, *Secularization of the European Mind*, 74, 86

time of Jesus Christ than it has in the last thirty years."[59] As I think about this, I realize that in this year my own grandmother was a young girl, and my great-grandparents were in their prime. Our family was full of painters and art-lovers. It may be hard for us to feel what they must have felt: they were witnessing the beginnings of modernism, while we are at its end.[60]

## The Crystal Palace

Perhaps, as Hughes suggests, the greatest metaphor for the coming of modernity was the Eiffel Tower. It was built in 1889, and was the center of the Exposition Universelle, a world's fair held in Paris. The challenge for the designers was to outdo the British Great Exhibition of 1851, all of which was housed in a great Crystal Palace in Hyde Park. Designed by Paxton, this astonishing structure was made almost entirely of glittering glass.[61] In it, Prince Albert sponsored Birmingham stoves, reciprocating engines and exotica from the colonies. How could the French

59. Quoted in Robert Hughes, *The Shock of the New* (New York: Knopf, 1991), 9.

60. The year 1913 was immensely significant in Western history and culture. Joseph Stalin published his first text, followed by his exile; income tax was authorized in the United States; the Mexican revolution occurred; Stravinsky's *Rite of Spring* was first performed; "Bloody Sunday" capped the Dublin lock-out; the New York Armory featured a show of modern art; and Camel cigarettes were introduced.

61. The Crystal Palace took eight months for construction, involved over 5,000 workers who handled more than 1,000 iron columns and 84,000 square meters of glass. All parts were prefabricated and easy to erect, and every modular unit was self-supporting, allowing the workers freedom in assembling the pieces. Over 18,000 panes of glass sheets were installed per week, and the structure was completed within five months.

outdo the British? By building upward, rather than further outward. Even today, reaching over 1,050 feet, the tower amazes us. But 130 years ago, it was truly astounding.[62]

## Delaunay, *The Eiffel Tower*

We now enter the twentieth century where much of this "progress" was celebrated in the arts. Consider Charles Delaunay's series on the Eiffel Tower (1909–1911). Reaching to the heavens, full of divergent colors, the red contrasting sharply with the gray of the surrounding buildings, it said something about the hope of the new, and the disappearance of the old order. Culture was reinventing itself at a great speed: an airplane crossed the English Channel, the machine gun was invented, as were synthetic fibers, the steam turbine, and the Kodak box camera.

## Léger, *The City*

Influenced by the chaos of urban spaces and his interest in brilliant, primary color, Fernand Léger sought to express the noise, dynamism, and speed of new technology and machinery often creating a sense of movement in his paintings that captured the optimism of the pre-World War I period.[63]

Matthew Affron explains:

> Léger attacked the Renaissance for a slavish imitation
> of nature that quashed aesthetic inventiveness and for a

---

62. The fair featured exhibits from all nations, and one could not miss the parallels with the Tower of Babel. In the old order, land was the most precious commodity. Now it was space, globalization, capitalism. Poets celebrated it and artists rendered it.

63. See http://www.theartstory.org/artist-leger-fernand.htm.

Léger, *The City*

Monet, *Haystacks*

Monet, *The Gare St-Lazare*

Monet, *Impression, Sunrise*

decadent preoccupation with official subjects and aesthetic hierarchies. This preoccupation, handed down as bad cultural education, had blinded subsequent generations to the truly dynamic and changing essence of beauty.

Léger, Affron further notes, maintained that "The Beautiful is everywhere; perhaps more in the arrangement of your saucepans on the white walls of your kitchen than in your eighteenth-century living room or in the official museums... There is a need for beauty scattered around the world... It is a question of a quantity and demand. It is a matter of satisfying it. Now I realize that we [artists] are still very useful 'as producers.'"[64]

## Bouguereau, *Thank Offering*

Whether this is a fair assessment of the Renaissance remains to be seen. But it is certainly true that the traditional sources for beauty, landscapes, mythological heroes, religious themes, were being pushed aside in favor of new sources. The old, the traditional, the religious, were becoming implausible. Here is the kind of art that was considered acceptable, academically sound in the nineteenth century. William-Adolphe Bouguereau (1825–1905) was an academic among academics. His work was pure, idealistic, sentimental, making him enormously popular during the time of Napoleon III. He painted a young girl who presumably had just been healed, gazing with her mother at the Virgin Mary, and lighting a votive candle.

64. Matthew Affron, Catalogue for Fernand Léger: Contrasts of Forms, Museum of Modern Art, New York, 1998, http://www.thecityreview.com/leger.html.

## Monet, *Impression, Sunrise*

An entire movement within the visual arts grew in the late nineteenth century. Much loved today, Impressionism, as it came to be known, was highly controversial at the time. As may be imagined, Bouguereau cordially disliked the Impressionists. They were indeed a revolutionary force within European art, opposing almost everything he stood for. A key figure in this revolution is Claude Monet (1840–1926). The name for the style he and a few others inaugurated, came about accidentally. When Monet was asked to give a name to an 1874 show in which a number of non-conformist artists exhibited their works, he suggested, quite casually, using the title of one of his contributions: *Impression, Sunrise*. Art critic Louis Leroy disliked the show and joked, "I am supposed to be impressed, so this must be an exhibit of impressionists." He meant to denigrate, but in fact he was saying something quite accurate. These painters wanted to depict not so much subjects as light itself. Anything would do: clouds, water, flowers. Art historian Denis Coutagne summarizes their goal:

> …what was in play in painting was light as a medium of dissemination and illumination… A shadow, for example, is no longer the absence of light which the painter uses in order to produce volume or relief or shape to what he is showing in full light, but the very refraction of light in its seemingly invisible blues, its ochres, its greens.[65]

How was this a secular move? For some time now the visual arts had been displaced from churches and chapels, and even

65. Denis Coutagne, *Cézanne abstraction faite* (Paris: Cerf, 2011), 107.

from homes, and placed instead in museums and galleries. Such a move is not in itself irreligious. Indeed, Protestant Christians had for some time argued for simplifying the worship arts and validating the calling of Christians outside the church. But where Monet and the Impressionists articulated a secular worldview was is in the transfer of the subject from heavenly, or transcendent motifs, to decidedly earthly ones. Eugène Delacroix counseled young artists to follow their hearts, not unlike the graduation speeches mentioned earlier. "Oh! Young artist, do you look for a subject? Everything is subject; the subject is yourself; it is your impressions, your emotions before nature."[66] Of course, Christians in the Van Tillian tradition can support the fact that everything, every object, every part of creation, is God-given. But that is not exactly what these painters were doing. They were somehow changing the center of gravity to objects below.

## Monet, *The Gare St-Lazare*

Not only the objects, but the way they were perceived made for a secularizing move. The radical change came when artists decided not to paint ideas but sense impressions. Like Delauney and Léger later, Monet was fascinated by the growth of modernity. Look, for example, at this rendering of the train station. We see black and white steam, tiny human figures, the powerful engine approaching, apartment building in the background designed by Georges-Eugène Haussmann to accommodate large masses of people. This is not Émile Zola's "Human beast," but Jean Renoir's "enchanted world of fairyland." The novelist Marcel Proust compares the train station and the

66. Quoted in Richard Schiff, *Cézanne et la fin de l'impressionisme* (Paris: Flammarion, 1995), 37.

departing trains to a liturgical instance, using words such as "mystery," "hope," and, "advent."[67]

## Monet, *Cathédrale de Rouen, plein soleil*

Even Monet's so-called religious subjects are quite secular. Consider his series on the *Cathedral of Rouen*. He made more than thirty of them in two years, each one showing the façade from different angles, in different seasons, at different times of day. He is not interested in the social or sacred function of the cathedral within a particular town. Apparently, he only actually entered the building once in the two years!

So, is Monet making any reference at all to the religious and cultural significance of a cathedral? Hard to say. Radical modern artist Casimir Malevich declared, "It is not possible to say that Claude Monet has reflected the bourgeois religious ideology, because Monet was working purely on variations in the physical light and not on the Cathedral of Rouen as such."[68] Was the cathedral, then, merely an occasion? Not likely. For Monet, as for most great artists, no motif is innocent.

## Monet, *Haystacks*

A better way of looking at Monet's choices is to suggest that Monet is profoundly aware of the value of the different worlds in the beloved country of France. The train station is the wonder of French engineering. The simple haystack honors the

67. Insights from *À la recherché du temps perdu*, vol. 1, p. 645, quoted and commented in Denis Coutagne, *Cézanne*, op. cit., 110.

68. Casimir Malevich, *De Cézanne au suprématisme* (Lausanne: l'Âge d'Homme, 1974), 103.

French peasantry. His Poplar trees denote to the beauties of the Normandy countryside. The cathedral surely represents the greatness of French civilization, impregnated by the Christian religion. In all this, however, Monet remains an Impressionist. His painting is not didactic. He marvelously renders a feeling. A feeling for country, a feeling for humanity, a feeling for the sacred. When we look at his paintings, we do not say, "Oh, how this looks like a cathedral, or a water lily." Instead, we gaze upon a nearly sacramental aspect of the surrounding context. "The stone becomes light. The light becomes paint."[69]

How does this signify secularization? Because, on the one hand, there is no real dependence on revealed truth, either general or special. Traditional religion, with its worldview, its institutions, its real presence, is functionally irrelevant. And yet, on the other hand, there is a sense of the "religious," a sense of spirituality, a higher value. Is such a sense necessarily opposed to traditional Christianity? We answer in the affirmative, because a truly biblical worldview is not vaguely spiritual but highly definite: beginning with the ontological Trinity, centered in the Incarnation, anchored in the verbal revelation of Scripture.

## An Ambiguity

Here we deal with an ambiguity. On the one hand, the arts, just like other human endeavors, look for spiritual meaning. André Malraux has argued that art is a fundamental response to a metaphysical reality. The reality to which art responds is "the fundamental emotion man feels in the face of life, beginning with his own."[70] And within that there certainly are

69. Denis Coutagne, *Cézanne*, op. cit., 115.
70. André Malraux, *La Tête d'obsidienne* (Paris: Gallimard, 1974), 221.

genuine expressions of Christian faith. Some noted Christians have boldly depicted a biblical worldview, as have, for example, Albert Gleizes and Georges Rouault. On the other hand, much of this "fundamental emotion" is anchored in what Robert Elliot Fitch used to call the "odyssey of the self-centered self."[71] Thus, in many portions of the visual arts, we observe this general secularizing shift away from revealed religion to a more earthly religiosity.

## Biblical Considerations

The point here is that despite some of the encouraging counter-trends, secularization is still with us. It may not be manifest exactly as the standard model had predicted. But it is present, drawing us in, not only by reasoned formulations, but by ambience, or plausibility. Nietzsche once put it this way: "What is now decisive against Christianity is our taste, no longer our reasons."[72] And yet, it turns out we are incurably religious. As Os Guinness astutely put it, "Religion is close to ineradicable in human nature, and strict secularism is finally unsatisfying for most people and even for secularists themselves."[73] Though many are returning to a biblical faith, secularization still skulks about.

This confirms Charles Taylor's diagnosis that secularization has come not only by subtraction (disenchantment, etc.) but by the availability of many options. Toward the beginning of his massive book on secularization, he announces his purpose

71. Robert Elliot Fitch, *Odyssey of the Self Centered Self; or, Rake's Progress in Religion* (New York: Harcourt, Brace & World, 1961).

72. Friedrich Nietzsche, *The Gay Science* (Cambridge: Cambridge University Press, 2001), 132.

73. Os Guinness, *Impossible People: Christian Courage and the Struggle for the Soul of Civilization* (Downers Grove: InterVarsity Press, 2016), 151.

in a question: "In a sense, the big question of what happened is, how did alternatives to the God-reference of fullness arise?"[74] For arise they have. In the smorgasbord of modern options, many choices and combinations are available to us. And yet, as Taylor also confirms, this will not lead to more freedom but to less.[75]

None of this should take Christians by surprise. According to Romans 1:18–23, God is not back: he never left! But yet we most often distort his truth and process the knowledge of him wrongly. Here is how Paul puts it:

> For the wrath of God is revealed from heaven against all ungodliness and unrighteousness of men, who by their unrighteousness suppress the truth. For what can be known about God is plain to them, because God has shown it to them. For his invisible attributes, namely, his eternal power and divine nature, have been clearly perceived, ever since the creation of the world, in the things that have been made. So they are without excuse. For although they knew God, they did not honor him as God or give thanks to him, but they became futile in their thinking, and their foolish hearts were darkened. Claiming to be wise, they became fools, and exchanged the glory of the immortal God for images resembling mortal man and birds and animals and creeping things.

The biblical take on the subject is that God continuously reveals himself to unbelievers and believers alike. This revelation is continuous.[76] And it is universally displayed. But it

74. Taylor, *A Secular Age*, 26.
75. Taylor, *A Secular Age*, 720.
76. The words translated "revealed" (v. 18), "is plain" (v. 19), and "clearly

is not properly received. Although at first, no one receives it, yet by the grace of God believers will embrace the free gift of righteousness in the gospel (Rom. 3:22).

When looked at closely, there are many examples of secularization in the Scriptures. Just as we have been setting it forth, the biblical examples divulge a dynamic process involving (1) the denial of revelation followed by (2) substitute religion. One of the most dramatic examples of this is Jeroboam's rebellion against the House of Solomon (1 Kgs. 12:25–33). Anxious to keep the kingdom from his rival Rehoboam, Jeroboam built cities in the north, as well as prohibited altars celebrating golden calves, and ordered worship to take place outside the prescribed calendar conducted by illegitimate priests. He told the people, "You have gone up to Jerusalem long enough. Behold your gods, O Israel, who brought you up out of the land of Egypt" (v. 28). Auguste Comte could not have done it better!

Such a dynamic becomes even more poignant in Paul's analysis of the local idolatry in Athens (Acts 17:22–34). The local people were providing food for local gods, in their little temples. But they were also worshiping an unknown god. There is a long history of the interpretation of this altar and of Paul's overall evaluation of pagan religion. I agree with Ned B. Stonehouse who says we have here not a path toward monotheism, but an open pantheon, which "like that of an open universe in which anything can happen, points to an underlying skepticism and irrationalism rather than to a movement

---

perceived," are in the present passive indicative, suggesting a reality, the things of God, received by human beings, making them responsible for the knowledge received.

towards the one living and true God."[77] Charles Taylor could not have said it better!

It is important to point out that secularization is not only an intellectual alternative, but an emotional one as well. Years ago, English poet and historian Matthew Arnold commented on Western civilization caught between a declining Christian culture and the false promise of a new one:

> Wandering between two worlds, one dead,
> The other powerless to be born,
> With nowhere yet to rest my head,
> Like these, on earth I wait forlorn.
> Their faith, my tears, the world deride —
> I come to shed them at their side.[78]

Notice the fatigue of the wanderer. The shift so well described by Charles Taylor is, among other things, wearying. This too is corroborated in the biblical accounts. Asaph records in Psalm 73 that while he was being buffered about by the injustices of the world, and before he entered into the temple, where he saw the world right-side up, he declared,

> "But when I thought how to understand this,
> It seemed to me a *wearisome* task" (v. 16).

The Hebrew word is `amal, which means toil, trouble, or labor. It is a great burden to be laboring in uncertainty and meaninglessness. The same word is used in the book of Ecclesiastes:

---

77. N. B. Stonehouse, *Paul Before the Areopagus, and Other New Testament Studies* (London: Tyndale Press, 1957), 14.

78. Matthew Arnold, *Stanzas from the Grand Chartreuse*, https://www.poetryfoundation.org/poems-and-poets/poems/detail/43605.

"Then I saw all the work of God, that man cannot find out the work that is done under the sun. However much man may *toil* in seeking, he will not find it out…" (Eccl. 8:17). Thus, secularity is not a brave new world of unshackled adventure, but a great burden, an affliction.

## CONCLUSIONS: A FEW ANSWERS

How then should we respond? It would be tempting to think the answer is simply to reverse this trend, and to re-enchant the world. All kinds of people are trying to do this, and there is some merit in that project. Consider, for example, those who are looking to re-mythologize the world, by reconnoitering Celtic culture. Numerous studies exist, from the engaging, *How the Irish Saved Civilization* to the more scholarly *Early Christian Ireland*, and the interest does not seem to be waning.[79] One of the freshest approaches which recognize the tenaciousness of Christian faith is Tom Holland's *Dominion: How the Christian Revolution Remade the World*.[80] Though brutally realistic about the problems created by the church, Holland deftly argues both for the positive influence of the Christian faith, and for the parasitic relation of evil movements to Christian themes.

Of course, there are skeptics and detractors.[81] And there are hundreds of ways to encourage more imagination and more good dreams. But the danger here is to present answers that are

79. Thomas Cahill, *How the Irish Saved Civilization* (New York: Anchor, 1996); T. M. Charles-Edwards, *Early Christian Ireland* (Cambridge: Cambridge University Press, 2000).

80. Tom Holland, *How the Christian Revolution Remade the World* (New York: Basic Books, 2019).

81. For example, Ian Bradley, *Celtic Christianity: Making Myths and Chasing Dreams* (Edinburgh: Edinburgh University Press, 1999).

hardly departures from secularization. They replace the emptiness but are the alternatives really different?

Faced, then, with secularization, whether hard or soft, I
suggest our message and our lives must carry a two-fold emphasis. First, the certainty of judgment to come. Paul preached
such a message to the Athenians. The times of ignorance are
ended. Next on the divine timetable is the dreadful day when
God himself, through his Son Jesus Christ, will expose all that is
on the hearts of people worldwide. He will expose the heart of
secularization which, to put it bluntly, is a lie. It's the deception
that makes us think we are merely alienated, in need of some
mysticism, whereas in fact we are morally corrupt, sinful rebels,
in need of the gospel.

The concept of God's judgment will not be welcomed by
most people today. And yet, many of them have a sense that
there should be an accounting. One even hears unbelievers say
things such as, "he will have a lot to answer for," and the like.
Secularization in all its forms cannot envision any kind of final reckoning. Despite its religiosity, it comes up empty. At the
heart of such emptiness is the absence of any real assessment,
any objective evaluation of the way things are. In his powerful argument for the certainty of a final judgment, the Apostle
Paul appeals to the awareness that each person has of right and
wrong (Rom. 1:28–2:16). But it is an awareness that makes us
culpable.

But now, second, our message must be the gospel. It is
still, as much as ever, the power of God to salvation (Rom.
1:16). Not only does receiving the gospel guarantee our safe
passage to heaven, but also this salvation includes every part of
human life. Just as secularization permeates every area, every
institution, every artistic vision, so the gospel applies to every
part of life. Models such as the culture wars are less than helpful.

For one thing, they give the impression that everything is easily identified with one side or another of a single battle. It is true enough that the great cosmic drama of human history is the ongoing conflict between the seed of the woman and the seed of the serpent (Gen. 3:15; Rom. 16:20). But for the moment the wheat and the weeds are growing up together (Matt. 13:30), and our task is not to identify white hats and black hats but to practice radical obedience to the rule of Christ in every sphere of life, the church, the home, the school, and the workplace.

Martin Luther famously wrote that the Christian is "lord of all, completely free of everything," and also "a servant, completely attentive to the needs of all."[82] By "lord of all," Luther does not mean we are above Christ, who truly is the King of kings and Lord of Lords (Rev. 19:16). He means that nothing can enslave us. And by servant he does not mean an unhealthy bondage to others. He quotes Paul from 1 Corinthians 9:19, which states that the Christian is free with respect to all, yet makes himself a slave to all at the same time (he also quotes Romans 13:8, Galatians 4:4, and Philippians 2:6–7, each of which explicates the love of neighbor).[83] This is the freedom we should propose to people of today. The service of God is perfect freedom, and the service of our neighbor is the perfect selflessness.

Only such a double posture can lead to a true alternative to secularization. Is it not strange, and wonderful, that the remedy for the blight of secularization is simply the two greatest commandments, enabled by the power of gospel? Is it not remarkable to remember, once again, that obedience to these overarching laws is only possible by the grace of God? For, as Luther himself, along with thousands of others, have discovered, such

82. Martin Luther, *The Freedom of a Christian*, trans. Mark D. Tranvik (1520; repr. Minneapolis: Fortress Press, 2008), 50.

83. Luther, *Freedom of a Christian*, 50.

righteousness is the gift of the justifier, through the redemption that is in Christ Jesus (Rom. 3:24).

The deepest need of our world is to return to the one true God. For what he wants for us is more than obedience to his law; he wants our fellowship with him. It is strange, but marvelously true: the God whose trust we have broken, whose curse is on the world, desires reconciliation with us. The ultimate remedy for secularization is not re-enchantment, but communion! Here is how Geerhardus Vos put it many years ago:

> To be a Christian is to live one's life not merely in obedience to God, nor merely in dependence on God, not even merely for the sake of God; it is to stand in conscious, reciprocal fellowship with God, to be identified with him in thought and purpose and work, to receive from him and give back to him in the ceaseless interplay of spiritual forces.[84]

---

84. Geerhardus Vos, "Hebrews, the Epistle of the Diatheke," in *Redemptive History and Biblical Interpretation: The Shorter Writings of Geerhardus Vos*, ed. Richard B. Gaffin (Phillipsburg: P&R Publishing, 1980), 186.

# The Heart of the Pastor and the Pulpit

R. Kent Hughes

# Introduction

Twenty-five years ago, an appendix in a book influenced the course of my life and ministry. I was a young husband and father, and a brand-new pastor looking for seasoned guidance on how to be who I was called to be. The book was *The Disciplines of a Godly Man,* by Dr. R. Kent Hughes, and the appendix surveyed books most recommended by many of the influential Christian leaders of that day. That appendix introduced me to a classic they all seemed to have read: John Calvin's *The Institutes of the Christian Religion*. Hughes's inclusion of that survey, to promote the godly discipline of reading, opened up a whole theological world for me and embedded the sense that men of God read!

The fact that such an appendix was included at all reflects something central to Hughes's more than a half-century of pastoral ministry. The disciplined stewardship of text and mind, heart and life, in the practice of ministry. The call to that stewardship is once again rung clear and loud in this lecture, delivered at the conclusion of Hughes's tenure as a visiting professor of Pastoral Theology at Westminster Theological Seminary. Here, Hughes calls preachers to give themselves to the engagement of head and heart as they devote themselves weekly to "twenty hours of holy, humble, rigorous, critical thinking" in the presence of God! The outcome of that sacred discipline should be an exegetically accurate, skillfully presented, Spirit-enabled, "blood earnest" proclamation of the "wholly inerrant, totally sufficient, and massively potent" Word of God from the heart of the preacher to the heart of the hearer. This was the message Dr. Hughes gave to his students week-in and week-out, month after month, in his few—but profoundly influential—years at Westminster. His lecture was something of a capstone to that relentless message.

The lecture was, however, more than an erudite academic farewell. It rang through with integrity of life and word. The content of this lecture characterized Hughes's ministry for five decades. His confidence in the sacred text of the Old and New Testaments was seen in his patient (and prolific) exposition of numerous biblical books. For Hughes, the text of Scripture is sovereign because the God of the text is sovereign. So, it was never enough on a Sunday to have an expositionally accurate, well-worded homily in front of him. He himself, as the preacher, had to be under the authority and message of the text—believing it from his heart and prepared to walk out its implications in his own life. That integrity of word and walk was daily demonstrated to the students and faculty of Westminster. Hughes infused a godly gravitas into each conversation and encounter, eliciting aspirations to Christ-likeness from pastoral students and inspiring the entire Pastoral Theology department to earnest stewardship in equipping the future pastors God had sent to us.

A quarter-century after I first read *Disciplines of a Godly Man*, I had the opportunity to meet the author and labor alongside him for a season. This afforded me the privilege of seeing, up close, Hughes's life and ministry as a man of God who preached from a heart formed in communion with God, with a mind renewed and reformed by studied exegesis of the Word of God, and driven by a God-given aspiration to reach the hearts of his hearers with the Word of God preached. That life and ministry is poured out on the pages of the lecture you are about to read. May God use it to inspire and instruct another generation to give their life to the exposition of God's "wholly inerrant, totally sufficient, and massively potent" Word!

John Currie
Winter 2020

# 2

# The Heart of the Pastor and the Pulpit

All that I will say today rests upon an expansive Reformed bibliology, which I regularly intone in my classes—that the Word of God is wholly inerrant, totally sufficient, and massively potent.

I've lectured and written about it elsewhere,[1] and I cannot do more than reiterate it here and add that having preached *lectio continua* for some fifty years, I am constantly amazed at the verbal and plenary inspiration of the Scriptures and am convinced that every word is inspired (every tense and connective), as is also the shape of the text, whether it be narrative, history, poetry, prophecy, parable, or compact *dominical dicta*, such as the Beatitudes and the Lord's Prayer.

I am convinced that every genre has its divinely shaped symmetries, and that the text's structure reveals the emphasis of the text. Beyond this, there is a Christological depth and cohesion throughout all of Scripture, which functions on the analogy of the human brain as it informs and coordinates the

1. R. Kent Hughes, "The Doctrine of Scripture and the Shape of the Sermon," in *Scripture and the People of God: Essays in Honor of Wayne Grudem*, eds. John DelHousaye, John J. Hughes, and Jeff Purswell (Chicago: Crossway, 2018), 265–69.

body. As Geerhardus Vos set forth in his inaugural address as professor of biblical theology at Princeton Seminary:

> In the Bible there is an organization finer, more complicated, more exquisite than even the texture of muscles and nerves and brain in the human body; that its various parts are interwoven and correlated in the most subtle manner, each sensitive to the impressions received by the others, perfect in itself, and yet dependent upon the rest, while in them and through them all throbs as a unifying principle the Spirit of God's living truth.[2]

This lecture also rests on the revelation of both the Old and New Testaments regarding the heart as being the center of human personality. "Heart," *leb*, in the Old Testament is used predominantly for the whole person—the seat of the spiritual and intellectual life, "the person in its totality,"[3] the place where one meets God. The New Testament use of *kardia* coincides with the Old Testament usage of the heart as the center of personality and clearly the place where God reveals himself.[4] The heart is the governing epicenter of the person.

Beyond that, what I'm going to say is grounded upon an understanding of the unity of the human person as represented by the use of "heart" in both Testaments—a unity that underlies Jonathan Edwards's thinking about the affections and religious experience. As Edwards scholar Gerald R. McDermott points out: "He [Edwards] rejected the threefold

2. Geerhardus Vos, *Inaugural Address* (New York: Anson D.F. Randolph, 1894), 40.

3. Colin Brown, ed., *The New International Dictionary of New Testament Theology*, Vol. 2 (Carlisle: Paternoster Press, 1975–1978), 181.

4. Ibid., 182.

distinction of mind, will, and emotion that became common in the nineteenth- and twentieth-century discussions of human psychology and in outline went back to Plato."[5] For Edwards, there exists no dichotomy in the human person that sets the mind against the heart or the intellect versus the affections. The person is a unitary whole. And it is on this unitary premise that I'm discussing the heart of the preacher and the pulpit.

## The Affections and Preaching

Of greatest importance is the condition of the preacher's heart and the work of the Holy Spirit within him as it relates to the text that he is preaching. It is a received fact that biblical exposition is enhanced when the preacher invites the Holy Spirit to apply the text he is preaching to his own heart and ethical conduct, so that the preacher is sympathetic to and humbly pursues the application of the text to his own life.

Phillips Brooks, the celebrated preacher and author of "O Little Town of Bethlehem," touched on this when he gave his famous definition of preaching in the 1877 *Yale Lectures on Preaching* when he said, "And preaching is the bringing of truth through personality"[6]—and then elaborated: "Truth through personality is our description of real peaching. The truth must come really through the person, not merely over his lips. . . . It must come through his character, his affections, his whole intellectual and moral being. It must come genuinely through him."[7]

5. Gerald R. McDermott, "Religious Affections," in *A Reader's Guide to the Major Writings of Jonathan Edwards*, eds. Nathan A. Finn and Jeremy M. Kimble (Wheaton, IL: Crossway, 2017), 99.

6. Phillips Brooks, *Lectures on Preaching* (Manchester, VT: James Robinson, 1899), 5.

7. Ibid., 9.

In the early 1900s, Methodist bishop William Quail carried the idea a bit further by asking a rhetorical question and then answering it: "Preaching is the art of making a sermon and delivering it? Why no, that is not preaching. Preaching is the art of making a preacher and delivering that."[8] These were helpful, ground-breaking observations, when qualified and not taken too far—at least not as far as Bishop Quail did when he concluded: "Therefore the elemental business in preaching is not with preaching, but with the preacher. It is no trouble to preach, but a vast trouble to construct a preacher. What then, in the light of this, is the task of a preacher? Mainly this, the amassing of a great soul so as to have something worthwhile to give— the sermon is the preacher up to date."[9] It seems that the bishop had been reading a bit too much of the rhetoricians, especially Quintilian's *Institutes*, which focused on sculpting goodness in the soul through a rhetorical education. (As an aside, John Calvin, who had been schooled in the twelve volumes of Quintilian, rejected Quintillion's thesis that goodness could come through the humanities, and co-opted Quintilian's title when he wrote *The Institutes of the Christian Religion*.[10] Evidently, Calvin thought that there was more to goodness than a liberal arts education.)

Bishop Quail seems to have forgotten, in his rhetorical enthusiasm, the Apostle Paul's transcending declaration, "for we do not preach ourselves" (2 Cor. 4:5). Indeed, many

8. William A. Quale, *The Pastor-Preacher* (New York: The Methodist Book Concern, 1910), 363.

9. Ibid.

10. Lester De Koster, "The Preacher as Rhetorician," in *The Preacher and Preaching: Reviving the Art in the Twentieth Century* (Phillipsburg: P&R Publishing, 1986), 19–22.

modern preachers do preach themselves with their practiced staging and their streaming of personal anecdotes and inner-directed explorations.

Nevertheless, Brooks is right. The truth of God's Word "must come through the preacher's character, his affections, his whole intellectual and moral being. It must come genuinely through him."[11] The necessity that the truth of God's Word must come genuinely through the preacher implies a looming professional danger, because it is possible for us preachers to imagine that we have spiritually been to places where we have never set foot. Brooks observed that in our repeated public proclamations of the grand truths of the faith, we can become like rail conductors of a bygone era who imagined that by announcing, "All aboard for Albany! All aboard to Chicago," that they had actually been there.

We can regularly urge our people to repent and grow so familiar with the doctrine of repentance that we are dulled to the fact that we ourselves are devoid of repentance.[12] C. S. Lewis saw the same thing in himself:

> Those like myself, whose imagination far exceeds their obedience are subject to a just penalty; we easily imagine conditions far higher than we have actually reached. If we describe what we have imagined we may make others, and make ourselves, believe that we have actually been there—and so fool both them and ourselves.[13]

11. Phillips Brooks, *Lectures on Preaching* (New York: E.P. Dutton and Company, 1877), 8.

12. Brooks, *Lectures on Preaching*, 25.

13. C. S. Lewis, *The Four Loves* (New York: Harcourt Brace & Company, 1960), 140.

Richard Baxter, the Puritan preacher par excellence, issued this memorable warning to preachers: "Lest they offer the bread of life to others which they themselves have not eaten."[14] So let us preachers be warned, as we live our days amidst the wonders of God's Word and the towering truths of divine revelation, that what we preach must come from and through our hearts. As John Owen said: "a man preacheth that sermon only well unto others which he preacheth itself to his own soul...If the word do[es] not dwell with power *in* us, it will not pass with power *from* us."[15]

However, nothing is more powerful than God's Word that is preached by one whose heart has been harrowed and sanctified by the Word he is preaching. The Puritan William Ames has it exactly:

> Next to the evidence of truth, and the will of God drawn out of the Scriptures, nothing makes a sermon more to pierce, than when it comes out of the inner affection of the heart without any affectation. To this purpose it is very profitable, if besides the daily practice of piety we use serious meditation and fervent prayer to work those things upon our own hearts, which we would persuade others of.[16]

14. This quotation is attributed to Baxter, but I have not been able to locate the source of the original words. The closest approximation I have found is in Richard Baxter, *The Reformed Pastor* (Edinburgh: Banner of Truth, 1994), 54–55.

15. John Owen, *The Works of John Owen,* ed. W. H. Goold (Edinburgh, 1853), 16:76

16. Art Lindsley, "Profiles of Faith, William Ames: Practical Theologian," *Tabletalk* (1983): 14.

## The Religious Affections

Theologically and practically, Jonathan Edwards, in his *Treatise Concerning the Religious Affections*, has given us the most nuanced explanation of what must take place within us. Edwards didn't use the word "affections," as we commonly do, to describe a moderate feeling of emotion or tender attachment. By "affections," Edwards meant one's heart, one's inclinations, and one's will.[17] Edwards said, "for who will deny that true religion consists in a great measure in vigorous and lively actings and the inclination of the will of the soul, or the fervent exercises of the heart?"[18] Edwards then goes on to demonstrate from a stream of Scriptures that real Christianity so impacts the religious affections that it shapes and animates one's loves, one's fears, one's hopes, one's hatreds, one's desires, one's joys, one's sorrows, one's gratitudes, one's compassions, and one's zeals.[19]

As to how the affections work? Edwards was very careful in defining "affections," as he described them as "springs" of motion—using the metaphor of springs of water to indicate how all human activity flows from the affections. "These affections," says Edwards, "we see to be the springs that set men a-going, in *all* the affairs of life, and engage them in *all* their pursuits." Take away the springs of motion, like love and hatred and hope and fear and anger, and the world would be stone cold, "motionless and dead."[20]

Religious affections do not function differently from nonreligious affections as well-springs of motion but have

17. Jonathan Edwards, *The Religious Affections* (Edinburgh: Banner of Truth, 1994), 24.

18. Ibid., 27.

19. Ibid.

20. John E. Smith, ed., *The Works of Jonathan Edwards*, vol. 2, *Religious Affections* (New Haven, MA: Yale University Press, 2009), 101.

radically different objects. Religious affections seek God and the things above. And, in concert with this, because religious affections involve, in Edwards's words, "lively actings" and "fervent exercises of the heart," they display themselves by springing up in active, fervent love for God with all one's heart and soul.[21]

Because the human self is unitary, as Edwards argued, so also are the affections—and the affection that overshadows and informs all of them is love.[22] Love is the well-spring of motion that buoys up all godly affections and actions. Therefore, when the preacher's heart overflows with love for God, all his affections (from his joys to his hatreds, from his gratitudes to his sorrows) will be attuned and energized to live passionately for the glory of God. And, when this is the case, the preacher's message will come through his whole intellectual and moral being in "lively actings" and "fervent exercises of the heart."

## Affectionate Preparation

For the preacher, what happens in the study when he sits down with the text before him—pulsing with its verbal and plenary glories—is of first importance.

### Twenty Sacred Hours

I have said this many times: "Sermon preparation is twenty hours of prayer"—because that is the amount of time that I have regularly needed to stand in the pulpit and deliver. So, understand that prayer envelopes all I say here.

21. Edwards, *Religious Affections*, 9.
22. McDermott, "Religious Affections," 101.

Sermon preparation is twenty hours of humble, holy, rigorous, critical thinking (in the presence of God!) about the text in its context. It is reading and re-reading the English text in the conscious presence of God, asking for wisdom to discern its theme, symmetries, and place in redemptive history. It is studying the text in the original Greek or Hebrew with lexicon in hand (without commentaries) so as to think for myself—circling the connectives and unusual words as well as concordant words, and defacing my text with lines and squiggles in a messy pursuit of discourse analysis. It is filling a legal pad with random thoughts about everything: from the context to applications, to cross references, to theological cruxes, to the text's structure and theme, to illustrations, and back to applications. And then, it is composing a tentative theme sentence (a central, integrating theme) and outline.

This done, I then open a respected commentary and discover that I got it all wrong!

I say all of this because getting the text right is serious business, because our theology and religious affections are determined by it. Precision in exegesis and homiletics is of cosmic importance.

## Heat and Light

Edwards clearly understood this and employed "light" as a metaphor for the truth of God's Word:

> Holy affections are not just heat without light; but evermore arise from some information of the understanding, some spiritual instruction that the mind receives, some light or actual knowledge. The child of God is graciously affected, because he sees

and understands something more of divine things than he did before, more of God of Christ, and of the glorious things exhibited in the gospel.[23]

A few sentences later, Edwards reinforces his point with Scriptures that link the love of God with such knowledge. Some of them are:

1 John 4:7, "and whoever loves has been born of God and knows God";

Phil. 1:9, "And it is my prayer that your love may abound more and more, with knowledge and all discernment";

Rom. 10:2, "they have a zeal for God, but not according to knowledge";

Col. 3:10, "the new self, which is being renewed in knowledge."

Edwards concludes: "Knowledge is the key that first opens the hard heart, [and] enlarges the affections."[24] So, it is the light of God's inerrant Word that is essential for elevating the heat of the religious affections.

## Imagination

And when it comes to preaching, the imagination of the preacher is crucial to helping his hearers to see the light of God's holy Word and thus raise the Fahrenheit of their affections. Edwards urged preachers to "stir up the pure minds

---

23. Edwards, *Religious Affections*, 281–82.
24. Edwards, *Religious Affections*, 281–82.

of saints, and quicken their affections by often bringing the great things of religion to their remembrance, and setting them in their proper colours."[25]

Yes, Edwards emphasized proper "colours." Edwards was insisting that preaching the great truths of the gospel must be imaginatively vivid (polychrome, so to speak), so that preaching captures and then elevates the imagination of the hearers. The famous example of this is his sermon "Sinners in the hands of an Angry God"—a sermon packed with astonishing "colours" (word pictures and metaphors) to convey the truth of God's Word.

Regarding the use of the imagination in preaching, Sinclair Ferguson posed this question: "How, through the work of the Holy Spirit, am I best to get the Word of God into the hearts of the people?" He then answered: "the one thing all of them seem to have in common is imagination—an imaginative creativity that bridges the distance between the truth of the Word of God and the lives of those to whom they speak."[26]

So, the hours of sermon preparation that I've recommended must be consciously infused with imagination. Yes, the exegesis of the Greek and Hebrew text in its context must be painstaking and precise, but the Word is Vossian-alive, and the imagination must encircle and illuminate the words and grammar of the text so that it is seen in exegetical, pulsing color.

The preacher must seek to understand the biblical text in its original horizon, say, of Corinth, Rome, Sinai, or Egypt.

25. Edwards, *Religious Affections*, 242.

26. Sinclair Ferguson, "Preaching to the Heart," in *Feed My Sheep: A Passionate Plea for Preaching*, ed. Don Kistler (Morgan, PA: Soli Deo Gloria, 2002), 209.

It is one thing to read up on the ancient culture, but it is another to invite the imagination to feel its textures and smell its aromas—to see young Joseph in Potiphar's house on the Egyptian Rivera where he awoke daily hearing chants to Osirus, to feel the oppression, to enter the perfumed presence of Mrs. Potiphar's temptation, to hear his ringing refusal as he invoked God's presence: "How could I do this thing and sin against God?" (Gen. 39:9). And, finally, to ponder Moses's narrative inclusion twice repeated at the beginning and the end of the account: "The LORD was with him" (Gen. 39: 2, 3, 21, 23). Yahweh/Emmanuel/Christ was with Joseph in the penthouse and now in the prison.

Imagination must inform our understanding of both the original horizon and the present-day horizon as the preacher imaginatively undertakes application. Much could be said about exercising cultural intelligence in making application—and the instruments are readily at hand through the print media and the internet so that not much imagination is required.

But the best way to understand the hearts of your listeners is to look into your own heart, and then your imagination will let you know where to go with your hearers. This reminds me of the quote often attributed to Turgenev: "I do not know what the heart of a bad man is like. But I do know what the heart of a good man is like, and it is terrible."

Finally, the writing of the sermon should be that of taking the great truths of the text you have exposited and, following Edwards, "setting them in their proper colours," and thus employing your imagination in creating the homiletic structure, using words, sentences, metaphors, and illustrations that truly enhance the preaching of the sacred text to the religious affections.

## Affectionate Proclamation

Jonathan Edwards believed that preaching is essential as it performs an indispensable function in reaching the heart. In Edwards's words, "[t]he impressing of divine things on the hearts and affections of men, is evidently one great end for which God has ordained, that his Word delivered in the Holy Scriptures should be opened, applied, and set home upon men, *in preaching.*"[27] He then goes on to say that while commentaries and books of divinity may be helpful, they do not have a power equal to preaching "to impress them upon men's hearts and affections."[28] He continues,

> God hath appointed a particular and lively application of his Word, in the preaching of it, as a fit means to affect sinners with the importance of religion…to stir up the pure minds of the saints, quicken their affections by often bringing the great things of religion to their remembrance, and setting them in their proper colours.[29]

So, Edwards calls for an affectionate proclamation of the Word, and that is what I will explore in this final section.

### Prayer

My own practice on the Lord's Day has been to rise early and get to my office so that I could spend two or three hours with the sermon—not memorizing it, but internalizing it by

27. Edwards, *Religious Affections*, 242
28. Ibid.
29. Ibid.

praying through its sections while asking myself, "Do I truly believe this?" and silently affirming that I believe it with all my heart. While focusing and affirming my affections, I also prayed that the Holy Spirit would help me bring the truth to my people, a prayer that I continued throughout the delivery. And sometimes I found myself offering inarticulate prayers of the "Lord, help me!" variety.

## Authenticity

Of primary importance is that the preacher be authentic—everything the preacher says is tinctured by what he is. As Tim Keller explains, "People do not simply experience your word, argument, and appeals as disembodied messages…They are looking for love, humility, conviction, joy, and power—for some integrity and congruence between what you are saying and what you are."[30] Therefore, it is essential that something has happened to your own heart and affections through the Word to ensure a congruence between your life and the truth that you are preaching from God's Word.

Certainly, the preacher must never imagine that he can fully embody or model the truth that he is preaching. Such imaginings would reveal the opposite. Nevertheless, he must be sympathetic to it and pursue it with his whole heart. William Ames's advice that we "use serious meditation and fervent prayer to work those things upon our own hearts, which we would persuade others of"[31] cannot be gainsaid. And when this happens, the sermon will come "out of the

30. Timothy Keller, *Preaching: Communicating Faith in an Age of Skepticism* (New York: Viking, 2015), 140.

31. Lindsley, "Profiles in Faith," 14.

inward affection of the heart without any affectation"[32]—with congruent authenticity and affectionate power.

## Passion

As to passion, Edwards called preachers to "an exceedingly affectionate way of preaching about the great things of religion and to flee a 'moderate, dull indifferent way of speaking.'"[33]

Certainly, ministering to the religious affections demanded passion. But it must be said that there was bogus passion in Puritan times just as there is today. I have known of a preacher who would run in place and jump up and down in the vestry so as to affect preacherly passion when he ascended the pulpit. I have been told of another who would stand on his head before appearing on the platform flushed and "full of the Holy Spirit." Method acting is the word for this.

However, false passion may have much subtler roots, as Dr. Martyn Lloyd-Jones observed of a preacher who prepares a message with which he is pleased and excited about its excellence: "It may be entirely of the flesh and have nothing at all to do with spiritual matters...You can be carried away by your own eloquence and by the very thing you yourself are doing and not by the truth at all."[34]

So, sinners that we preachers are, we must be wary of ourselves and the source of our homiletical passion. No marginal notations: *Weak point here—raise voice. Weaker point— pound pulpit!*

32. Ibid.

33. C. C. Goen, ed., *The Works of Jonathan Edwards*, vol. 4, *The Great Awakening* (New Haven: Yale University Press, 1972), 386.

34. D. Martyn Lloyd-Jones, *Studies in the Sermon on the Mount* (Grand Rapids: Eerdmans, 1976), 2:183.

Despite abuses, the Scriptures know of and call for a godly passion. As Paul told the Thessalonian church, "our gospel came to you not only in word, but also in power and in the Holy Spirit and with full conviction" (1 Thess. 1:4). The full conviction was not the conviction that the Thessalonians experienced, but Paul's full conviction as he preached the Word to them in the power of the Holy Spirit. That was the way he continued to preach and exhort the church in every quarter as he told the Ephesians, "that for three years I did not cease night and day to admonish everyone with tears" (Acts 20:31). That was also Jesus's way on occasion. Can anyone imagine that his lament over Jerusalem was muted and dispassionate? "O Jerusalem, Jerusalem, you who kill the prophets" (Matt. 23:37). No, it was a loud, wailing lament!

Biblical preaching evokes passionate delivery that flows from the conviction that what you are preaching is true. Where there is no passion, there is no preaching. That said, we must also realize that the display of passion must be requisite with your God-given personality. There are some people, like the nineteenth-century Scottish elders, who are (by nature) so subdued that if they raise their left eyebrow and a corner of their mouth twitches, they are figuratively rolling in the aisles!

It is a matter of historical record that though Edwards had "an exceedingly affectionate way of preaching," he sometimes never gestured, or even moved. At the same time, his was not "a moderate, dull, indifferent way of speaking." Serano Dwight—the fifth son of Yale University president Timothy Dwight and pastor of Park Street Church in Boston, Massachusetts—offered the following thoughts after listening to an unanimated sermon by Edwards:

If you mean by eloquence the power of present-
ing an important truth before an audience, with
overwhelming weight of argument, and with such
intenseness of feeling that the whole soul of the
speaker is thrown into every part of conception and
delivery....Mr. Edwards was the most eloquent man
I ever heard speak.[35]

Edwards's passionate eloquence was requisite with his
God-given personality.

To further the point, the celebrated Scottish preacher
Thomas Chalmers, according to James Stewart, preached
"with a disconcertingly provincial accent, with an almost total lack of dramatic gesture, tied to his manuscript, with his
finger following the written lines." His secret? His "blood
earnestness."[36] A universe of homiletical wisdom is con-
tained in those two words.

However we preach, we must do so with "blood
earnestness. J.W. Alexander, in his *Thoughts on Preaching*,
argues that the preacher must be himself in regard to
preaching: "There is a certain type of thought, diction,
and delivery, which is proper to each individual; and he
accomplishes most who hits on this. But all straining, all
artifice, and all imitation tend to prevent the attainment of
this manner."[37] In this vein, Alexander remarks: "No man
can be a great preacher without feeling...but feeling cannot
be produced to order: and the affectation of it, however
elegant, is powerless." He adds, "Where there is more voice,

35. John Piper, *The Supremacy of God in Preaching* (Grand Rapids: Baker
Books, 1976), 49–50.
36. J.W. Alexander, *Thoughts on Preaching* (Edinburgh: Banner of Truth,
2009), 264.
37. Ibid., 30.

more emphasis, more gesture than there is feeling, there is waste, and worse."[38] The spirit of the copyist is blind because he imagines that by latching on to the intense style of an admired preacher he will enjoy the same effect. This is the mistake that want-to-be John Pipers have been making for decades. Imitating Piper's pulpit postures, cadences, gestures, vocabulary, expressions, and passionate style will not replicate his ministry.

Apart from a preacher's unique gifting, the key to his ministry lies in his religious affections. According to Brooks, "There is nothing more beautiful than when the truth of God's Word comes through the preacher's character, his affections, his whole intellectual and moral being." As Ames remarks, "nothing makes a sermon more to pierce than when it comes out of the inward affection of the heart without any affectation." And what about passion? "It is always beautiful when it is well employed; that is to say, when it is artless and flows from the heart."[39]

## The Holy Spirit

The preaching, as well as the preparation, must be an exercise in full dependence upon the Holy Spirit. A tall ship might be loaded with treasure (your well-prepared sermon), but it will go nowhere unless the wind fills its sails. Only the wind of the Spirit can blow the treasures of Scripture into the harbors of men's hearts.

As I mentioned earlier, that is why I would rise and be in my office two to three hours before the first service

38. Alexander, *Thoughts on Preaching*, 30.

39. Alexandre Vinet, *Homiletics; or, The Theory of Preaching*, trans. Thomas H. Skinner (New York: Iveson & Phinney, 1854), 460.

to prayerfully go through my sermon in slow-motion, in conscious dependence upon the Holy Spirit as the one who empowers preaching, convicts the world of sin, and upholds righteous judgment. After my sermon preparation, as I preached, I prayed in the same dependent vein.

## Affections

As to the preaching event itself, Edwards declared it his duty to elevate the religious affections of his congregation: "I should think myself in the way of duty, to raise the affections of my hearers as high as I possibly can. . . . Our people do not so much need to have their heads stored, as to have their hearts touched; and they stand in need of that sort of preaching which has the greatest tendency to do this."[40] Edwards further believed that the preaching event (the existential time of proclamation), was crucial, stating that "the main benefit that is obtained by preaching is by the impression made upon the mind in the time of it, and not by the effect that arises afterwards by a remembrance of what was delivered."[41]

In our own time, Dr. Martyn Lloyd-Jones concurred: "The first and primary object of preaching...is to produce impression. It is impression at the time that matters, even more than what you can remember subsequently." He added, "Edwards, in my opinion, has the true notion of preaching. It is not primarily to impart information.... We are not merely imparters of information. We should tell our people

40. Jonathan Edwards, *Some Thoughts Concerning the Present Revival of Religion in New England* in *The Works of Jonathan Edwards* (Edinburgh: Banner of Truth, 1974), 1:391.

41. Edwards, *Some Thoughts*, 1:397.

to read certain books themselves to get information there. The business of preaching is to make such knowledge live."[42]

The elevation of affections is key to effecting change. Our contemporary Tim Keller, who, like Lloyd-Jones, is noted both for his cerebral approach to exposition and his ministry to modern skeptics from the pulpit, agrees in principle and practice: "[P]reaching to the heart can change people right in their seats. A sermon that just informs the mind can give people things to do after they go home, but a sermon that moves the heart from loving career or acclaim or one's own independence to loving God and his Son changes listeners on the spot."[43] This is what happened to Serrano Dwight when he heard Jonathan Edwards preach—"impressions were made that could not be effaced."[44]

The preacher must preach with Edward's driving goal of "impressing…divine things on the hearts of men." The preacher must elevate the affections to change the lives of the hearers. Here I must re-emphasize our unitary nature, and the fact that when the affections are moved, our whole being is moved (animated) toward the beauties of Christ and toward the fruits of the spirit. This must be the goal of every preacher.

## Christ

Of course, the transcending end of all preaching must be to exalt Christ—to preach the text treading the redemptive-

42. D. M. Lloyd-Jones, *The Puritans: Their Origins and Successors: Address delivered at the Puritan and Westminster conferences 1959–1978* (Edinburgh: Banner of Truth, 1976), 360.

43. Timothy Keller, *Preaching: Communicating Faith in an Age of Skepticism* (New York: Viking, 2015), 165.

44. Piper, *Supremacy of God in Preaching*, 50.

historical axis from Genesis to Revelation, making the inter-canonical connections declaring the dazzling manifestations of Christ and preaching him from our hearts to the hearts of our people.

And as to the hearts of us preachers? Sinclair Ferguson puts it memorably: "the personalities of the preachers of the cross must be marked by the cross. So we are called to be cruciformed (shaped by the cross), Christophers (bearing the cross of Christ) and Christplacarders (setting Christ and him crucified on display)."[45]

45. Ferguson, "Preaching to the Heart," 217.

# Gregory of Nazianzus:
## The Pastor as a Physician of Souls

Alfred J. Poirier

# Introduction

The Christian life is a struggle. A striving after truth not only in the *theory* of our doctrine and life, but a striving after truth in the *practice* of it. Not for this endeavor alone, but, through faith in Christ, to know him and the power of his resurrection, straining forward to what lies ahead, pressing on to make it our own because Christ has made us his own (cf. Phil. 3:8–14). It is in this spiritual struggle and straining forward that we encounter our own sin and brokenness as well as the sin and brokenness of others. The struggle against sin begins in the innermost heart and continues in the outworkings of everyday life. Such a struggle, then, takes a special kind of care, not of outward issues or only externals, but one that addresses and meets the spiritual and inner struggle of sin. The foundation of such care begins in the heart of God and is revealed in his promises made and promises kept. Promises kept like John 10:11, "I am the good shepherd. The good shepherd lays down his life for the sheep," and promises made like in Jeremiah 3:15, "I will give you shepherds after my own heart." In John 10, first we meet Christ, our great shepherd, and in Jeremiah 3, God's Christlike shepherds.

It is precisely here at the intersections of inward sin, outward strife, God's grace, and congregational life that both Gregory of Nazianzus and Alfred Poirier consider the pastoral care of souls. Gregory of Nazianzus famously remarked in his *Second Oration*,

> The goal of our art is to provide the soul with wings, to rescue it from the world and give it to God, and to watch over that which is in his image, if it abides, to take it by the hand, if it is in danger, or restore it, if ruined, to make Christ dwell in the heart by the Spirit: and in short to deify and bestow heavenly bliss upon, one who belongs to the heavenly host.[1]

Poirier likewise has urged in his *The Peacemaking Pastor* this ministry of reconciliation since:

> As pastors and church leaders, then we need to be and must be intimately a part of the lives of our people. We cannot flee from reality; we cannot fear involvement. We cannot avoid conflict. For we do not want to preach and counsel mere words; we want to preach and counsel the living Word. When our words are disconnected from the hardships of life, from the conflicts of heart and home, we become mere purveyors of knowledge, not pastors.[2]

1. Gregory of Nazianzen, *Oration* 2.22, in Philip Schaff and Henry Ware, eds., *Nicene and Post-Nicene Fathers: Second Series* (Grand Rapids, MI: Eerdmans, 1989), 209.

2. Alfred Poirier, *The Peacemaking Pastor: A Biblical Guide to Resolving Church Conflict* (Grand Rapids, MI: Baker Books, 2006), 21.

No pastor and faithful under-shepherd could or would claim that they improve upon God's design for the pastoral ministry. Instead, like signs pointing to the true destination and the reality beyond them, these two pastors and theologians enrich our understanding of the pastoral ministry as it has been laid forth by Christ.

I hope you will take the time not only to reflect on what is mentioned here, but I believe you will be blessed and fortified, if, after reading this lecture, you would go back to Gregory of Nazianzus's *Second Oration* and Alfred Poirier's *The Peacemaking Pastor.* They are helps and guides to encourage towards Christ. For just as God promised shepherds after his own heart, Christian pastors must be gripped by the call of Christ that he is the good shepherd laying down his life for the sheep.

Christian, consider how we must follow Christ's example of the cross, even through the death to self and life to God. Pastors and seminarians, consider the great and glorious calling that is before you in the pastoral care of souls, that "art of arts and science of sciences."[3] Or as Alfred has said,

> For a church to become a true peacemaking church, renewal must start in the hearts of the leaders by their hearing afresh the Good News that our God is a God who raises the dead—even dead pastors. Once we as leaders are gripped by this gospel of peace, we can call our churches back to biblical peacemaking,

3. Nazianzen, in *NPNF 2*, 208.

leading from weakness, not strength—or better yet, leading by God's strength revealed in our weakness (2 Cor. 12:9).[4]

May the Lord be pleased to make his glory known!

Todd M. Rester
Winter 2021

---

4. *The Peacemaking Pastor,* 269.

# 3

# Gregory of Nazianzus:
# The Pastor as a Physician of Souls

Are we not here today to train pastors to proclaim the gospel of our Lord Jesus Christ, in accord with the whole counsel of God, and in keeping with his call for us to be true physicians of souls?

For that reason, I thought it most appropriate to offer an appreciation of the ministry and message of the man who coined that singular phrase "physician of souls," even Gregory of Nazianzus.

Of course, that phrase is adapted from our Lord Jesus's own words, who said: "Those who are well have no need of a physician, but those who are sick. I have not come to call the righteous but sinners to repentance" (Luke 5:31).

I would seek to do three things: First, to give a thumbnail sketch of the man and his life. Second, to recall the profound and lasting effect he made on pastoral ministry through his *Second Oration, In Defense of His Flight to Pontus* (*Or.* 2).[1] And

1. Gregory Nazianzen, "Oration II, In Defence of his Flight to Pontus, and his Return, after his Ordination to the Priesthood, with an Exposition of the Character of the Priestly Office," in *Select Orations of Saint Gregory of Nazianzen*, in *S. Cyril of Jerusalem, S. Gregory Nazianzen*, eds. Philip Schaff and Henry Wace, trans. Charles Gordon Browne and James Edward

third, to engage more directly with his *Defense* in the terms he set down, asking and answering three questions:

  1. Why did he flee the ministry (2.1–15)?
  2. What does a pastor do, and what kind of man should a pastor be (2.16–94)?

And finally,

  3. Who is the man worthy of this call (2.95-117)?

So first, briefly, the man and his life.

## The Man and His Life

Gregory was born in 329 AD and died in 390. He lived in that tumultuous century of change where the church went from being persecuted, to tolerated, to becoming the official religion of the Empire.[2] One might surmise that

---

Swallow, vol. 7, A Select Library of the Nicene and Post-Nicene Fathers of the Christian Church, Second Series (New York: Christian Literature Company, 1894), 204–228. Daley notes the following, "The title given to Oration 2 varies in the Byzantine manuscripts but is usually some variant of the following: 'An apologetic Discourse of Saint Gregory the Theologian, on Account of his Flight to Pontus and Return from There, because of his Ordination as Presbyter; in which the Subject is: What the Nature of the Priesthood is, and what kind of Person a Bishop should be.'" See Brian E. Daley, S.J., *Gregory of Nazianzus* (New York: Routledge, 2006), 206n210. Hereafter, citations for Gregory's *Orations* are abbreviated *Or.* and are to be found in *Select Orations of Saint Gregory of Nazianzen*, 203-436.

  2. Beginning with the Emperor Constantine's Edict of Milan in 313, the Edict of Toleration, to his calling of the church's first ecumenical council in Nicaea in 325, and concluding with the Emperor Theodosius's the Edict of Thessalonica (*Cunctos populos*) in 380.

the church had finally conquered paganism, but we would be grossly mistaken. For the battle with paganism simply turned inward. In becoming the Empire's church, it now embraced and welcomed a multitude of people with a myriad of unchristian elements.[3]

It was during this century that Gregory was born, lived, and loved his Lord, and served God's church as pastor, preacher, poet, and theologian. Though the middle child, Gregory was the first son born and thus named after his father, Gregory the Elder.

His father had been converted from paganism to saving faith in Christ through the gentle witness of his wife. And in quick succession, Gregory the Elder was ordained and then appointed Bishop of Nazianzus.[4]

Now, while Gregory held both his father and his mother in highest esteem, his greatest affection was reserved for his mother, Nonna. Why? Well, it was she who had come from a long line of devout, Cappadocian Christians. It was she who won her husband to Christ. It was she who cultivated in Gregory a deep love for the Lord.

Indeed, elsewhere he calls her the "ἀρχηγός" or "spiritual leader"(*Or.* 18.6–7),[5] "the very mouth of truth" (*DVS*

3. Brooks Otis, "The Throne and the Mountain," *The Classical Journal*, Vol. 56, No.4 (January 1961): 146–47.

4. See Gregory Nazianzen, *Saint Gregory of Nazianzus: Three Poems: Concerning His Own Affairs, Concerning Himself and the Bishops, Concerning His Own Life,* ed. Thomas P. Halton, trans. Denis Molaise Meehan, vol. 75, The Fathers of the Church (Washington, DC: The Catholic University of America Press, 1987), 2.

5. "Oration 18: Funeral Oration On His Father, In the Presence of S. Basil," in Gregory Nazianzen, *Select Orations of Saint Gregory Nazianzen,* in *S. Cyril of Jerusalem, S. Gregory Nazianzen,* ed. Philip Schaff and Henry Wace, trans. Charles Gordon Browne and James Edward Swallow, vol. 7, A Select Library of the Nicene and Post-Nicene Fathers of the Christian

64).[6] To her, he credits his own passion to know and love God through his Word and to strive to be a faithful teacher of Scripture (*DVS* 95–100). Little wonder that he would later write some thirty-six epitaphs for her alone.[7]

And it is to Nonna that Gregory attributes one of the most formative influences on his life, and that was her dedication of him to the Lord before his birth. For you see, both Gregory the Elder and Nonna were advanced in years when they began to have children. And seeing that their first child, Gorgonia, was a daughter, and thinking she may never have a son (like Hannah of old), Nonna pleaded to the Lord to grant her a son and promised to dedicate him for service in his church, if the Lord would grant her request (*Or.* 18.11).[8]

And indeed, he did. The Lord gave Nonna a son, even Gregory. And that sense of destiny, of having been set apart

---

Church, Second Series (New York: Christian Literature Company, 1894), 254–69.

6. *De Vita Sua* (Concerning his Own Life), in *Saint Gregory of Nazianzus: Three Poems*, 75-130. Hereafter, abbreviated *DVS* and cited in the text.

7. Brian Dunkle, "Introduction," in *Poems on Scripture: English Translation*, ed. John Behr, trans. Brian Dunkle, vol. 46, Popular Patristics Series (Yonkers, NY: St. Vladimir's Seminary Press, 2012), 12.

8. *Or.* 18.11 "Funeral Oration on His Father, in the Presence of S. Basil." Gregory Nazianzen, "Oration XVIII, On the Death of the Fathers," in "Select Orations of Saint Gregory Nazianzen," in *S. Cyril of Jerusalem, S. Gregory Nazianzen*, ed. Philip Schaff and Henry Wace, trans. Charles Gordon Browne and James Edward Swallow, vol. 7, A Select Library of the Nicene and Post-Nicene Fathers of the Christian Church, Second Series (New York: Christian Literature Company, 1894), 257–58. See also, *Or.* 2. Nonna's dream is recorded in *De rebus suis,* 424–466; see *Saint Gregory of Nazianzus: Three Poems*, 39.

before birth to serve the Lord in his church made an indelible mark on Gregory all the days of his life.

What of you? Who in your life was most formative for encouraging you to pursue God's call on your life? A mother like Nonna? A father? A friend? A teacher? A mentor?

Who of us can say that we stand here today on our own? Rather, are we not here today because the Lord gave us many fathers, mothers, friends, and teachers who encouraged us on to greater love for Christ and service for him?

O, give thanks to the Lord for such friends and teachers!

## Karbala

Now, Gregory's family were wealthy landowners of a fine estate in Karbala, ten miles southwest of Nazianzus in the Roman province of Cappadocia, Asia Minor, what is today modern Turkey. For most of his life, this family estate would be his place of refuge and repose.

Wherever he might go, whether to Athens (the Harvard or Cambridge of the day) where he studied for ten years and became a renowned rhetor, or to Pontus where he fled from the ministry soon after he was ordained, or to Seleucia (*DVS* 526-46)[9] for a lengthy and needed retreat after having to bury, in the short space of five years, every member of his immediate family: first his brother, Caesarius (369), then his sister Gorgonia (370?), then his father (374), and finally his mother (374); or whether he went to Constantinople to pastor the little church Anastasia (Resurrection) and preach the doctrine of the Trinity in the face of great opposition (for all

9. See also John A. McGuckin, *Saint Gregory of Nazianzus: An Intellectual Biography* (Crestwood: St. Vladimir's Seminary Press, 2001), 225–27.

the churches there were governed by anti-Nicene clergy);[10] wherever he might go, Gregory always returned to Karbala, to his family home, his refuge.

And there he spent his final years, compiling his correspondence of some 249 letters, composing 17,000 lines of poetry and hymns (not a few for teaching the young the Bible and biblical truths);[11] and there he edited his forty-four orations, among which was his *Second Oration*, his *Defense of His Flight to Pontus*.[12]

Now, time does not permit us to tell how he, who as one of the Three Great Cappadocians Fathers, helped craft the language we now use to speak of the mystery of mysteries—the Holy Trinity.[13] Nor can we delve into the conflicts he experienced as a pastor, first in Nazianzus, and later in Constantinople, where on Easter Day, as he prepared new converts to be baptized, an unruly crowd of anti-Nicenes attacked his church, destroyed the altar, and hurled stones at him.[14]

10. See Gregory of Nazianzus, *On God and Christ: The Five Theological Orations and Two Letters to Cledonius*, ed. John Behr, trans. Frederick Williams and Lionel Wickham (Crestwood, NY: St.Vladimir's Seminary Press, 2002). See also *Or.* 42.2.

11. See Brian Dunkle, *Poems on Scripture*, 35–157.

12. For his letters, see Bradley K. Storin, trans., *Gregory of Nazianzus's Letter Collection: The Complete Translation* (Oakland: University of California Press, 2019).

13. W. C. Weinrich, "Gregory of Nazianzus," in *Evangelical Dictionary of Theology: Second Edition*, ed. Walter A. Elwell (Grand Rapids: Baker Academic, 2001), 526. See also Christopher A. Beeley, *Gregory of Nazianzus on the Trinity and the Knowledge of God: In Your Light We Shall See Light* (New York: Oxford University Press, 2008), 187–233.

14. See *Ep.* 77, "To Theodore of Tyana," in Storin, *Gregory of Nazianzus's Letter Collection*, 93. See also *DVS* 654–65; *Concerning Himself and the Bishops* 103.

Nor can we linger over the time when, soon after, a young man attempted to assassinate him, even as Gregory lay sick in bed.[15]

Yes, this is the pastor I would have us consider today: he who served for a brief time as the President of the Council of Constantinople in 381; he whom the Eastern Church has honored since the Council of Chalcedon in 451 with the title "The Theologian."[16] Indeed, it is no exaggeration to say that what Augustine is to us in the West, to the East is Gregory.

So now, having something of a glimpse of the man and his life, let us consider briefly the impact Gregory had on pastoral theology by way of his *Second Oration*, or his *Defense*.

## In Defense of His Flight to Pontus

Gregory's *Defense* consists of 117 paragraphs or sections, which, in our English translation, total to a little over 19,000 words.[17] And one of the first things that strikes anyone who reads it, or anything else of Gregory's, is that he "bleeds Scripture."[18]

In his *Defense* alone, there are over 430 specific Bible verses cited or phrases used: 243 from the Old Testament and 195 from the New Testament.[19]

15. This was after Theodosius appointed him patriarch of Constantinople. See *DVS* 1440–1474; Gregory Nazianzen, *Saint Gregory of Nazianzus: Three Poems*, 117–118. See also, *Or.* 33.5.

16. McGuckin, *Saint Gregory of Nazianzus*, 393.

17. I arrived at this figure by copying the oration from *NPNF*, then ran a word count on a word processor. This is in only a rough estimate and only on the English translation. Nevertheless, it is a sizeable treatment.

18. The phrase is often attributed to a remark of Spurgeon about John Bunyan, whereby he said: "Cut him and he bleeds Scripture."

19. Figures are drawn from Brian Matz, *Gregory of Nazianzus*, yet his count differs from mine. See Brian Matz, *Gregory of Nazianzus* (Grand Rapids: Baker Academic, 2016), 73–74.

Secondly, in no small measure is the significance of his *Defense* due for having been the first pastoral theology of the church. Prior to this work, the church had only the scattered remarks on pastoral ministry as found in the New Testament (the Pastoral Epistles) and in a handful of early church orders (like the *Didache*), and letters and commentaries by various early fathers.[20]

Yet, Gregory's *Defense* gave the church one of the most sustained and substantive works on pastoral theology that continues to bear much fruit even after 1600 years.[21] Besides being the first biblical, theological treatise on pastoral ministry, it provided the blueprint for John Chrysostom's own similar work titled *Six Books on the Priesthood*, written near the end of Gregory's life.[22]

Then, almost two hundred years later, in 590, Gregory the Great composed his own work titled *The Book of Pastoral Rule*, which itself became the definitive book on pastoral theology for the next thousand years, and wherein at the very beginning of his work, he acknowledges his own debt to Gregory the Theologian.[23]

20. Church orders such a *Didache, Apostolic Tradition, Didascalia, Apostolic Constitutions;* Letters, such as Ignatius's letters; Commentaries, such as Origin's *Commentary on Matthew* 16.19. For the development of thought on pastoral ministry in the early centuries, see Claudia Rapp, *Holy Bishops in Late Antiquity: The Nature of Christian Leadership in an Age of Transition* (Berkeley: University of California Press, 2005), 24–41.

21. Christopher A. Beeley, *Gregory of Nazianzus on the Trinity and the Knowledge of God: In Your Light We Shall See Light* (New York: Oxford University Press, 2008), 237. Beeley calls it "his most developed single treatment of the ministry."

22. See Claudia Rapp, *Holy Bishops in Late Antiquity,* 41–42. See also St. John Chrysostom, *Six Books On the Priesthood,* trans. Graham Neville (Crestwood: St. Vladimir's Seminary Press, 1977).

23. See John T. McNeill, *A History of the Cure of Souls* (New York: Harper

Now, we are not to think that Gregory's *Defense* was delivered *viva voce*. Most likely, it was published at the time of his return, and in later years received considerable editing by him.[24] Yet, for all that Gregory accomplished, and for all the accolades received both during and after his life, what may surprise us is to note how inauspicious a beginning he had in pastoral ministry. So let us press on to the main subject—and consider in some detail the *Defense* itself.

## Gregory's Flight

First, recall the circumstances of its composition. In Christmastide of 361, Gregory the Elder, now seventy-five years old and weakening, ordained his namesake son to church office. Days later, Gregory fled. That's right. Though he had just been ordained a pastor, preacher, and shepherd, he fled—he fled his church, his people, Christ's flock, and his home.

---

& Row, 1951), 108–109; see also George E. Demacopoulos, "Introduction," in St. Gregory the Great, *The Book of Pastoral Rule*, trans. George E. Demacopoulos (Crestwood: St. Vladimir's Seminary Press, 2007), 9–25.

24. McGuckin, *Saint Gregory of Nazianzus*, 106–107. Beeley, *Gregory of Nazianzus*, 237; see also Browne and Swallow, "Prolegomena," in *NPNF*, Series 2, vol. 7, 194. Gregory likely gave *Or.* 1 and 3 *viva voce* which themselves contain not only his reason for his flight, but the nature of the pastorate. We should not think of Oration 2 as Gregory's sole work concerning the pastorate, for the subject never leaves him. He appears to have thought long and often on pastoral life, care, and leadership as is evident elsewhere in his works. See his extended comments on the ministry in *Ors.* 9–13 (372) when made Bishop of Sasmia; also, see *Ors.* 18, 21, 24, 43, when writing biographies of other great pastors such as his father, Cyprian, Athanasius, and his friend Basil. And in *Or.* 6, 22, 2, his three *Orations on Peace*, as he sought pastors to reconcile their differences and unite over orthodox teaching on the Trinity.

He fled to Pontus, where together he and his dear friend, Basil the Great, consoled each other as they considered the consequence of ordination (*Or.* 43). After a few months, by Easter of 362, Gregory had returned home and resolved to assume the office from which he fled. And having returned, he set about to write this *Defense* to explain to his congregation the reasons for his previous actions.

As you will recall, he does so by asking and answering three questions: First, why did he flee the ministry? Second, what does a pastor do, and what kind of man should a pastor be? Third, who is the man worthy of this call?

Let us take each in turn.

## Why Gregory Fled the Ministry
## (Or. 2.1–15)

So first, why *did* he flee the ministry? Was he a coward? Was he rebelling against the imposition of it by his father? Were there other reasons for his flight? Gregory quickly dismisses these allegations. He is no coward and no rebel. But he does admit that his ordination startled him. He says he reacted to it as one does to hearing a "sudden noise" (*Or.* 2.6).

Elsewhere, he describes his reaction to ordination as like an "ox stung by a gadfly," and like such an ox, he lost control of his reasoning and acted impulsively (*DVS* 350).

Now, who of us wouldn't admit that at times those more challenging responsibilities of pastoral office tempt us, if not to flee the ministry, at least to eschew certain pastoral duties? For some, that may be avoiding counseling a difficult member, or searching out an unruly one. For others, the temptation may be to evade the labor of prayer and reflection; and still for others, shirking the difficult task of preparing a sermon that actually feeds God's flock?

Whatever the reasons, at times we do flee. And so did Gregory.

Yet, Gregory alludes to a more significant reason for his flight. He longed for the contemplative life. He longed to shut himself off from the world that he may know God, rather than to be, as he says, "thrust into the midst of a life of turmoil" (*Or.* 2.6)—a most adequate expression of pastoral ministry. All his life, Gregory wrestled with this tension between life alone with God and life in service to God in his church.

In a subsequent oration (*Or.* 12, c. 372), Gregory speaks about this life-long tension, and his inner struggle between these two poles, these two desires. On the one hand, he desires to know God, to read, pray, sing, and study God's Word; and then, on the other, he desires to serve others in Christ's church. So he says:

> The one suggests flights, mountains and deserts, and calm of soul and body... in order to hold pure communion with God...The other wills that I should come forward, and bear fruit for the common good, and be helped by helping others; and publish the Divine light, and bring to God a people for His own possession, a holy nation, a royal priesthood (1 Pet. 2.9), and His image cleansed in many souls.

He concedes the latter is the better. Why? Because, he says: "...as a park is better than and preferable to a tree, so also, in the sight of God, is the reformation of a whole church preferable to the progress of a single soul..." Then he reminds us of our Lord who did likewise:

> For Christ also...when it was possible for him to abide in His own honour and deity, not only so

far emptied Himself as to take the form of a slave (Phil. 2.7), but also endured the cross, despising the shame (Heb. 12.2), that he might by His own sufferings destroy sin, and by death slay death (Heb. 2.14). (*Or.* 12.4)

Who of us cannot appreciate that same struggle? Did not our own father in the faith, John Calvin, long to lead the quiet life of a scholar until Farel got ahold of him?[25]

Gregory never found balance or reconciliation between these twin desires. And I think few of us have or will. Eventually, though, Gregory comes to the real reason why he ran from the pastorate. Can you guess by now why he fled? His answer is simple: "I did not, nor do I now, think myself qualified to rule a flock or herd, or to have authority over the souls of men" (*Or.* 2.9).[26]

Not qualified? Think of it, argues Gregory. If it is hard to learn to submit to leaders, and harder to learn how to rule over men, to guide men to God is the hardest task of all (*Or.* 2.10). Indeed, as Gregory confesses: "For the guiding of man...seems to me in very deed to be the art of arts and science of sciences" (*Or.* 2.16).

Do you believe that? Do we believe that the pastoral ministry, the guiding of men to God is "the art of arts and the science of sciences"? I dare say the world doesn't. And too often neither does the church.

25. See Calvin's preface to his commentary on the Psalms. John Calvin and James Anderson, *Commentary on the Book of Psalms*, vol. 1 (Bellingham: Logos Bible Software, 2010), xlii–xliii.

26. See also *Or.* 2.78 where Gregory admits that he is unqualified to lead his people and refers to problems in ministry where the title "priest" was an empty word.

We want to have capable men to pastor our churches—have them conduct our religious services, lead a nice bible study, hold the hand of the sick here, preach a sermon there, and make sure our children have fine nurseries and our youth are cared for. But do we regard the calling of a pastor and his labor as nothing less than the practice of "the art of arts and the science of sciences"? I fear not. And Gregory fears not too.

Furthermore, he knows that many who hear these words, "the art of arts and the science of sciences," will think them mere hyperbole. So, at this point in his *Defense*, Gregory leaves off from offering reasons for his flight, and sets himself to the task to prove his assertion by demonstrating what is actually entailed in being a pastor who practices this "art of arts and the science of sciences." And he does this simply by asking us to reflect with him as to what task a pastor does, and what kind of man he should be.

## What Does a Pastor Do and
## What Kind of Man Should He Be?
## (Or. 2.16–94)

To answer this question, Gregory begins with a picture. He holds out before our eyes the image of two physicians. One is a physician of the body and the other a physician of souls. And he calls on us to compare and contrast these two vocations (2.16).[27]

For clarity, I shall speak of these different vocations as between a doctor and a pastor. Gregory points to three major differences:

First, doctors and pastors differ in terms of their subject

27. See also *Or.* 2.18–19, 24.

matter (2.16–21). One is concerned with the physical body, the other with the soul.

Secondly, they differ in terms of the ends for which they labor (2.22). One deals with prolonging human life, the other with matters of eternal destiny.

Third and finally, they differ in terms of the power of the science each employs (2.23–25). One appeals to medical science while the other ponders the mysteries of God and the gospel of his Son.

Let's take each in turn.

(1) Doctors and pastors differ in terms of their subject matter (2.16–21). Gregory is not unaware of how difficult a doctor's calling is.[28] A doctor must scrutinize a patient's age, season, time and place, and only then can he apply the proper medications or treatments (2.18). Indeed, Gregory allows that at times a doctor's treatment may indeed need to be severe. A doctor may need to burn or cut away what is infected. Think today of some of the more severe treatments doctors must employ to help heal us, such as chemotherapy or open heart surgery, or an organ transplant.

Yet, argues Gregory, however laborious and hard these are for a doctor, they cannot compare to what is required of a pastor. For, though a pastor too must make a diagnosis, unlike the doctor, notes Gregory, a pastor must deal with the "habits, passion, lives, and wills," of souls (2.18). And consider this, adds Gregory: doctors apply their treatments to the body, wherein, for the most part, the patient is relatively passive and docile.

Is this the case for a pastor, the physician of souls? Not at all, he states. Instead, how often does the pastor find

---

28. Let us not forget that his brother, Caesarius, was a capable physician, even serving in the court of the emperor. See *Or.* 7, esp. 7.8.

that his godly counsel is not only not heeded but received with open rebellion and opposition, "amounting almost to an armed resistance" (2.19). He goes on: think how people "hide away their sins," allege excuses, devise pleas in defense of their failings, close their ears to godly counsel, and even, "shamelessly brazen out their sin before those who would heal them" (2.20).

And this "struggle," this "wrestling," as Gregory depicts the pastor's work, highlights yet another way in which the subject matter between doctors and pastors differ (2.17). Doctors deal with the surface matters of the person's body, whereas pastors investigate "the hidden man of the heart, and our warfare is directed against that adversary and foe within (2.21).

"For these reasons," he argues, "I allege that our office as physicians far exceeds in toilsomeness, and consequently in worth, that which is confined to the body" (2.21).

Yet, this is only the first way in which doctors and pastors differ.

Gregory continues with the second difference. Doctors and pastors differ not only to the respective *subject matter*, the body for the one, the soul for the other, but—

(2) Doctors and pastors differ also in terms of the ends for which they labor (2.22, 27–28).

Ask yourself: Whether as doctors or physicians of souls, what is our final goal?

Consider a doctor's end goal. What is it? To preserve a life, to heal the flesh. A doctor helps a man that he may "live some days longer on the earth." But even then, asks Gregory, "How long will he be able to live? Forever?" (2.27). Of course not.

But now consider the final goal to which a physician of souls labors. What is the end of all our wrestling, struggle, and warfare with the hidden man of the heart? What is the end of all our sleepless nights and tears as we labor to lead men to God? Is not the end of our labor "the salvation of a soul, a being blessed and immortal, and destined for undying chastisement or praise" (2.28)?

Did not our Lord Jesus say as much when he told us that there will be more joy in heaven over one sinner who repents (Luke 15)? Can that be said of the development of the latest vaccines? Or, of Apple's new iPhone? Or Elon Musk's electric car? Or Jeff Bezos's goal to fly us back to the moon? Of course not! Though these may be the news makers of our day, none of them can compare to the end, the goal for which we labor—the salvation of souls.

Do we pastors, professors, and students believe this?

Or, do we at times lose sight of that goal for which Christ has called us, and consider our labors, whatever they may be—giving a devotion, praying for the sick, counseling an anxious heart, or delivering a sermon—as a thing insignificant?

Let us never forget that every time our tongues proclaim the glorious gospel of the Son, we are in truth God's instrument, in God's hands, guiding souls from wrath to grace, raising people from death to life, leading men from utter darkness into the light of blessed communion with the Holy Trinity. Or, as Gregory says, leading souls to their Bridegroom (2.77)!

And thus, says Gregory: "...the scope of our art is to provide the soul with wings, to rescue it from the world and give it to God..." (2.22).

So, doctors and pastors differ in terms of their subject matter and differ as to their ends. Yet, there remains one final difference which is the greatest difference of all:

(3) Doctors and pastors differ in terms of the power of the science each employs (2.23–25).

What does Gregory have in mind by that?

By "power of the science," Gregory means the knowledge or truth that *effects real change.* For instance, what is the "power of science" to which a doctor must apply himself? Is it not to the entire field of medical knowledge and practice?

Think of it. What does a student doctor study? Is it not anatomy, physiology, histology, microbiology, chemistry, pathology, neurology, and many other needful sciences? And all this knowledge in which a doctor seeks to be conversant is applied in the hope of effecting real change in the bodies he seeks to help.

But what is the "power of science" for the physician of souls, the pastor? What "power of science" must you as a physician of souls apply yourself to know that you may employ such science to lead others to God? Is it not the very mysteries of God, the mysteries of the gospel of his Son?

Indeed, it is. "This is why," answers Gregory, "

God was united to the flesh...why the new was substituted for the old...why Jesus was baptized...and was tempted...why devils were cast out, and diseases healed....This is why the heathen rage and the peoples imagine vain things; [this is] why tree is set over against tree...This is the reason of the lifting up to atone for the fall...and of death for death, and of darkness for the sake of light, and of burial for the return to the ground, and of resurrection for the sake of resurrection. (*Or.* 2.23–25)

Let us pause and ask: Do you see better now the reason why you are preparing for the ministry? Is it to know better, and deeper, the glorious mystery of the gospel of God's Son, the mystery of his incarnation, life, obedience to death, resurrection, ascension, and promised return?

Is not this the reason that sustains you in the dark night of the soul? That supports you when you stumble? Is it not this grand mystery of Christ's humiliation and exaltation that ought to awaken you and revive and move you to continue your ministry each day, to keep steadfast in the fight, as you labor to lead others to God?

Let it be. O, let it be.

Having lifted our hearts, then, to peer into the bright mystery of mysteries, the science of sciences, having compared and contrasted in these three critical ways the differences between a physician of the body and a physician of souls, Gregory now directs us back to consider the manifold skills and wisdom required for pastoral practice.

He notes first how great a diversity of people God has called us to care for. Men and women, young and old, rich and poor, sanguine and despondent, sick and whole, rulers and ruled, wise and ignorant, married and unmarried, what a mixture of tempers and temperaments that tests the best of pastors and demands us not to treat everyone in the same manner (2.28–29).

Then, Gregory continues noting that not only must we care for different *kinds* of people, or those at different stations in life, or those with differing capabilities, but, as he observes, we must care in the differing ways that people allow themselves to be led. Observe, says Gregory, that "Some are led by doctrine, others trained by example; some need the spur, others the curb" (*Or.* 2.30).

And after considering such a diversity of care, Gregory comes to what he calls "the first of our duties" (*Or.* 2.35). Do you know what he means by that? He means the public and private proclamation of God's Word!

In quick succession, he traverses the essential doctrines that we pastors need to teach: our original constitution and final restoration; the types of the truth (in the Old Testament); the covenants; the first and second coming of Christ; incarnation, sufferings and…resurrection; the last day; the judgment; and to crown all…the supreme and blessed Trinity (*Or.* 2.36).

Moreover, argues Gregory, if we are charged to instruct others positively, we ourselves must avoid every heresy and false doctrine. And surely, have not our own days been fraught with similar false teachings?

Was not Westminster Seminary founded in the face of the Modernist movement wherein false pastors and leaders sought to cast off the very fundamentals of our faith: the infallibility of God's Word, the deity of Christ, his virgin birth, his miracles, his atoning death, his resurrection from the dead, his second coming, and the final judgment?

And are we not still wrestling today over these and many other truths? Have we not had to wrestle in our day with attacks on justification by grace alone through faith alone; the denigration of penal substitutionary atonement; the denial of the doctrine of creation, and of man as male and female; the doctrine of marriage as designed by God for one male and one female for life; and all manner of confusion in the area of sexual ethics?

Indeed, we have.

And shame on us pastors who, though teaching sound doctrine, fail to warn and strengthen our congregations against the errors of our enemy where he is most fierce today in the fight.

Having then set forth the first of our duties in the positive proclamation of God's Word, and the need to guard against heresies, Gregory returns again to his earlier concern, now not asking what a pastor does, but what kind of man a pastor should be. And he begins here with the prince of pastors, the Apostle Paul.

Recalling Paul's ministry, Gregory says:

> [I]...set forth Paul as the witness to my assertions, and for us to consider by his example how important a matter is the care of souls... I say nothing of his labours, his watchings, his sufferings in hunger and thirst, in cold and nakedness, his assailants from without, his adversaries within. I pass over the persecutions, councils, prisons, bonds...the daily and hourly deaths... (*Or.* 2.52–53)

And yet, in all this, says Gregory, Paul does not boast in himself, but rather, "He glories in his infirmities and distresses. He takes pleasure in the dying of Jesus, [2 Cor. 4.10; 12.9, 10]" (*Or.* 2.55). And seeing this sufficient, Gregory concludes, asking, "Why should I enter into detail? [Paul] lived not to himself, but to Christ and his preaching. He crucified the world to himself..." (*Or.* 2.56).

Who of us cannot see what Gregory is doing? Is he not displaying before our own eyes, even as the Apostle Paul many times did, the *cruciformed* character of pastoral life and by it commending the same to us again?

What does it mean for us to be a pastor? It means *to die with and for Christ*. Did not Bonhoeffer echo the same, saying: "When Christ calls a man, he bids him come and die."[29] Did you ever tell that to someone who asked you: "Why do you go to seminary? Why enter the pastorate?" Did you tell them the reason? Do you tell them the nature of Christ's call on you? Do you answer: "I chose seminary, and the pastoral call, because Christ called me to come and die"?

And leaving off with Paul, Gregory goes on to canvas the great pastors God has given the church and how each, in their own day, stood against the tide of the world. He surveys quickly the ministries of Isaiah, Hosea, Joel, and all the other prophets and notes throughout how each in their own generation had to contend for the faith.

But then Gregory pauses with Ezekiel. Here, he sums up the Lord's accusations against the shepherds in Ezekiel 34 (*Or.* 2.64). Do you recall that passage? Let us listen to what our Lord said to Israel's Shepherds:

> This is what the Sovereign Lord says: Woe to you shepherds of Israel who only take care of yourselves! Should not shepherds take care of the flock? You eat the curds, clothe yourselves with the wool and slaughter the choice animals, but you do not take care of the flock. You have not strengthened the weak or healed the sick or bound up the injured. You have not brought back the strays or searched for the lost. You have ruled them harshly and brutally.

Does not our Lord's word prick our souls with conviction, moving us to ask: In what ways have I despised the

29. Dietrich Bonhoeffer, *The Cost of Discipleship* (New York: Simon & Schuster, 1995), 89.

ministry? In what ways have we pastors or professors been well fed, but neglected to feed Christ's sheep, eating the curds but failing to strengthen the weak, clothing ourselves with wool, but not healing the sick, not bringing back the strays, not seeking the lost, and instead ruling harshly?

Have we taken up ministry of the Word like pastors or peddlers? Are we seeking to prepare for the pastorate simply as a means to make a living or to gain man's approval, rather than to care for Christ's flock?

Brothers and sisters, let it never be said of us that we treated the holy things of God as things merely common.

Gregory has asked two questions. He asked, why did he flee the ministry? And he answered that he did not think himself qualified to rule a flock (*Or.* 2.9). And he asked, what does a pastor do and what kind of man should a pastor be? And answered that a pastor practices the art of arts and science of sciences as a physician of souls—not living for himself but for Christ as he leads others to God (*Or.* 2.16).

Now, having laid out before our eyes the scope and nature of this high and heavenly calling of God, Gregory asks the third and final question: Who is the man?

## Who is the Man?
### (Or. 2.95–117)

Who is the man worthy to take up this call of God?

> Who is the man...who hearkens but pays no heed to these names... the titles and powers of Christ?... God, the Son, the Image, the Word, the Wisdom, the Truth, the Light, the Life, the Power...The Maker, the King, the Head, the Law, the Way, the Door...

the Peace, the Righteousness...the Servant, the Shepherd, the Lamb...the Firstborn before creation, the Firstborn from the dead, the Resurrection... Who...is the man who, although he has never applied himself to, nor learnt to speak, the hidden wisdom of God in a mystery...yet will joyfully and eagerly accept his appointment as head of the fulness of Christ? (*Or.* 2.98–99)

And, as if throwing up his hands in defeat, shattered and subdued by the immense weight of God's call to the pastorate, Gregory finally answers: "No one...no one is worthy" (*Or.* 2.95–99). *No one is fit to be a pastor* (*Or.* 2.99)!

And yet, Gregory acknowledges that someone must care for Christ's flock. Someone must answer God's call, for the Lord has called men to pastor and help the weak and lead them to God. Moreover, Gregory, though he fears to take up this call, trembles far more at the thought of not answering: "For it is to be feared," says he, "that we shall have to hear these words concerning those who have been entrusted to us: 'I will require their souls at your hands'..." (*Or.* 2.113).

And with that, Gregory steps forward, however unfit he is and unworthy to pastor. He steps forward and answers God's clear call on his life; and like Isaiah of old ends his *Defense*, saying: "Here am I, my pastors and fellow-pastors, here am I, thou holy flock, worthy of Christ, the Chief Shepherd..." (*Or.* 2.116).

## Conclusion

Well, here I am, and I have run my course too. I trust this brief appreciation of Gregory of Nazianzus, this pastor and *physician of souls,* has not only humbled us by the grand vision of the glory and weight of the task God has called us to bear in the ministry, but equally may it strengthen you to know that he who commands supplies. He who calls gives.

Let us all together humble ourselves before our Triune God, confess our many failings, and renewed in heart put our hands to the plow, and, as those raised with Christ, set our eyes on him in whose name Gregory blesses, saying:

> May the God of peace…
> the Shepherd to shepherds and a Guide to guides:
> that we may feed His flock with knowledge,
> so that in His temple everyone,
> both flock and shepherds together may say,
> Glory, in Christ Jesus our Lord,
> to Whom be all glory for ever and ever.
> Amen (*Or.* 2.117).

# WESTMINSTER

THEOLOGICAL SEMINARY

EST. 1929

**Master of Divinity**
**Pastoral Fellows**

"Designed for the making of a pastor"

At Westminster, we are committed to offering the profound preparation necessary to equip the next generation of pastors to faithfully serve Christ's church for a lifetime. For more than 90 years, Westminster alumni have served around the world as pastors and church leaders, grounded by a deep understanding of the Whole Counsel of God, with a heart to serve in the midst of the daily and cultural challenges of their unique contexts.

**Inquire now for more information:**
**wts.edu | 267-579-2366**

# WSP✝

Westminster Seminary Press (WSP) was founded in 2011 by Westminster Theological Seminary in Philadelphia, Pennsylvania. WSP is a uniquely Reformed academic publisher dedicated to enriching the church, the academy, and the Christian through the printed word. WSP collaborates widely—including with faculty, staff, and students at Westminster—to publish new and classic books that foster faith in and obedience to Jesus Christ from an orthodox, Reformed per- spective. For more information, visit www.westminsterseminarypress. com, email wsp@wts.edu, or write to us at 2960 Church Road, Glenside, Pennsylvania 19038.